THE VICTORIAN SEASIDE COOKBOOK

Anne Bishop
&
Doris Simpson

New Jersey Historical Society

Library of Congress Catalog Card Number 83–061979
ISBN 0-911020-09-8
Printed in the United States of America

THE
VICTORIAN
SEASIDE
COOKBOOK

Published with Funds from
Friends of the Society,
the E. J. Grassmann Trust,
and an
Anonymous Gift
Dedicated to the Memory of
Delia Brinkerhoff Koster

CONTENTS

To Our Mothers
Selene Brien Rowan
and Hazel Kraemer Schwing
With Love and Gratitude

INTRODUCTION

THE *Victorian Seaside Cookbook* has been inspired by the fabulous hotels of the New Jersey's shore area from 1860 to 1901. The distinctive cuisine of Atlantic City, Long Branch, and other seaside resort communities has been preserved in the old hotel menus found in the collections of the New Jersey Historical Society; Special Collections, Alexander Library, Rutgers University; the Atlantic City Free Public Library; and the Atlantic County Historical Society. By finding contemporary Victorian recipes for the best of the wide variety of dishes listed in the menus, comparing different versions of the same recipe, then carefully testing and adapting each, a modern cookbook has been created.

Atlantic City boardwalk and lighthouse, 1875.

The Jersey Shore has long attracted visitors seeking the health and entertainments offered by the seaside. After the American Revolution, it became popular with well-to-do Philadelphians to board with local folk at the Jersey Shore. Before long, boarding houses were established in Long Branch and Cape May that catered to summer visitors. The two-to-three day journey by wagon or stage was onerous, and many visitors preferred traveling to the seaside communities by sailing sloop and later by steamboat. After the first quarter of the nineteenth century, regular steamship routes to Long Branch and Cape May brought visitors from New York, Philadelphia, Baltimore, Washington, D.C., and points south, all wishing to escape the discomfort and hazards of the summer season in their growing cities.

Demand for accommodations soon warranted the construction of a few large hotels. This demand mushroomed after the middle of the nineteenth century, when a network of railroad lines to key shore points was opened with the completion of a line from Camden to Absecon in 1854. Relatively short, comfortable, and inexpensive travel by railroad soon made the Jersey Shore a popular vacation place. Realizing this, the railroads published promotional literature extolling the virtues of various shore communities. They not only spurred the growth of existing resorts like Long Branch but made possible the development of entirely new areas like Atlantic City.

Victorian era vacationers had a host of choices for their sojourn at the Jersey Shore. During the second half of the nineteenth century, New Jersey seaside resorts multiplied, all vying for the tourist trade. Land developers sang the praises of the salubrious climate, the broad expanse of beaches, the local seafood, game and farm produce, and the opportunities for sport fishing and hunting. Generations of "summer folk" were lured by the Jersey Shore's well-cultivated reputation for seaside recreation and gastronomic delights—for days at the races and nights with high society. And shore promoters also preached the benefits of quiet, secluded vacations at Methodist camp meetings in communities that strictly observed the Sabbath and anti-liquor ordinances.

Vacationers could stay in large hotels, boarding houses, elegant private homes, or even tents. But the Jersey Shore's finest accommodations were the large, well-staffed hotels, offering the latest in amenities, by the standard of the day. Evening balls, theatricals, concerts, billiard rooms, croquet grounds, gambling salons, and elegant dining augmented the simpler seaside pleasures. Long Branch's Ocean Hotel and West End Hotel and Cape May's Congress Hall and Stockton House became the places where one could see and be seen. Illustrious political, theatrical, and social figures of the era stayed at the Jersey Shore hotels. Presidents Ulysses S. Grant, James A. Garfield, Benjamin Harrison, Grover Cleveland, and William McKinley frequented the shore. So did personalities of some notoriety such as "Boss" Tweed, Lillian Russell, and "Diamond Jim" Brady. While Cape May's status as the Jersey Shore's most fashionable resort declined after the Civil War, as patronage by the South's wealthy planter class waned, Long Branch thrived and rivaled Saratoga, New York's glamorous spa, as the summer watering place of the wealthy and powerful. Atlantic City's ascendancy was to come toward the end of the century.

The menus of the dining rooms of the large and popular hotels reveal much about the eating habits and tastes of Americans in the Victorian era. These were years of tremendous technological progress that influenced the quality and availability of food and revolutionized food preparation and consumption by Americans. In 1862 President Abraham Lincoln signed two bills that heralded the beginnings of this new age. One bill, the Morrill Act, led to the establishment of state agricultural colleges; the other, the Pacific Railway Act, led to the construction of a transcontinental railroad. With the implementation of these acts came improved farming methods, new and improved breeds of livestock, and the development of improved grains and vegetables, together with the means to transport them to all parts of the country. These, along with new milling techniques, improved leavening agents, the pasteurization, condensation, and evaporation of milk, and the development of the refrigerated railroad car made it possible for Americans to enjoy food of a quality and variety never before known. Visitors to the Jersey Shore in particular revelled in the availability of fresh New Jersey produce and plentiful seafood.

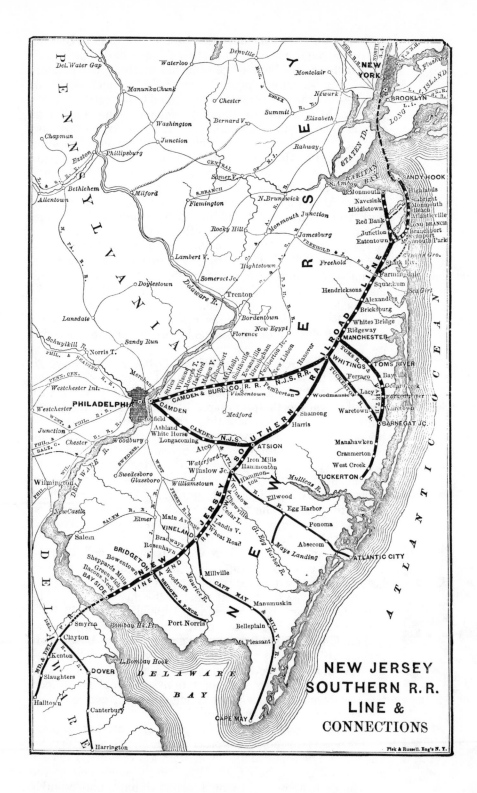

A railroad map of lines servicing the Jersey Shore, 1873.

Queen Victoria may have set the tone for the era bearing her name, but food—and most other things—had to be French to be fashionable. So, a simple dish like stuffed green peppers could only be called "poivres verts farci." French words or phrases, idiomatic or ersatz, were added to pedestrian dishes in order to give them a touch of elegance. The result was menus filled with such unlikely offerings as porterhouse steak au onions, apple fritters glassé au rhum, and Hamburg steak au prué. The French influence also served to upgrade the menus with classic dishes such as poulet à la Marengo and blanquettes de veau. But for those guests who looked askance at all this Gallicizing, there was still traditional fare: pork and beans, bread pudding, corned beef and cabbage, rice pudding, boiled beef, and other such homely vittles.

The menus also reveal the Victorian penchant for excess, as obvious in their dining as it was in their dress and furnishings. The number of courses offered, the seemingly endless train of dishes served at each course, and the amount of food expected to be consumed is nothing short of staggering. What follows is a description of the sorts of meals served at the Victorian shore hotels based on surviving menus.

During the Victorian era the hearty breakfast was de rigueur. To the Victorian mind, the sight of a properly attired family seated at a heavily laden breakfast table was a sure sign of moral worth and prosperity. The menus of the Jersey Shore hotels clearly reflect this Victorian attitude. A typical breakfast might begin with a large assortment of fruit, followed by clam broth, then a hot cereal. (Around the turn of the century, cold cereal such as shredded wheat began to appear in response to the campaign of health-food advocates.) Then would follow three or four kinds of fish from which to choose. The morning feast continued with grilled steaks, lamb chops, liver, eggs cooked to order, creamed codfish or beef, ham and bacon, several varieties of potatoes, hominy, and fried mush. There were also griddlecakes served with honey or maple syrup. All of this was accompanied by hot chocolate, coffee, tea, milk, or malted milk.

Luncheon was the lightest meal of the day and was to be eaten five hours after breakfast. Typically, it would have started with a soup, followed by fish served with potatoes and cucumbers. Next would come a meat or meat-based dish, served with a choice of potatoes and vegetables. Cold sliced meat would be offered, along with a salad, followed by simple desserts such as ice cream with assorted cakes and perhaps watermelon. The meal concluded with coffee or tea served with crackers and cheese.

It was for dinner that the full glory of Victorian culinary genius was reserved. The typical dinner had several services and parts. The first usually began with a shore specialty such as oysters on the half shell—blue points were considered the choice oyster—or littleneck clams in particular months. Next came the soup course, offering either a clear soup or a thick soup. In the early Victorian shore menus, soup appeared as the first course. (The hors d'oeuvre course, often missing from the menus, ideally would have followed; it would have consisted of both hot and cold dishes.) Then came the fish course for which two kinds of fish were offered, a boiled or braised fish and a broiled or fried fish.

The relevée (the main meat course) was next, comprising a solid joint of meat, or poultry, and two vegetables. This meat course was followed by the entrées ("made dishes"), which were usually meat- or fish-based selections accompanied by a vegetable. Though unusual to modern tastes, the entrée might also have been a sweet dish such as fritters, puffs, or farina cakes, napped in a light, sweet sauce. Then came a ten- or fifteen-minute interval when the table was cleared and punch or sherbet was served. If only men were present, cigars might be passed around.

The roast course was served next. Game was the preferred roast, but any meat or poultry might be served. Cold meats, accompanied by a salad, followed the roast. The most popular salads at the Jersey Shore hotels were hearty varieties such as chicken, lobster, or potato salad. In 1886, when President Grover Cleveland and Frances Folsom were married in the White House, a lettuce-and-tomato salad was served at their wedding luncheon. This salad became immensely popular and appears often on the shore menus.

Next came the sweets. A large variety of desserts, both hot and cold were offered. Hot sweets such as puddings and pies were served first, followed by the cold dishes such as blancmange, creams, jellies, Charlottes, and cakes. These desserts were topped off by selections of fruits, nuts, cheeses, and confections. Coffee and cordials completed the dinner. Throughout the meal appropriate wines were served with each course, though proper ladies were expected to sip the wines and never to drain the glass.

Supper was served as the evening meal, usually between 6:00 and 7:00 P.M., on those days when dinner was eaten at midday. Supper was also fashionably served between 11:00 P.M. and 1:00 A.M. during an evening of dancing or other entertainment. Typically, the hot dishes served were oysters prepared in four or five different ways, broiled steak, chops, ham and bacon, fried fish, and eggs, variously prepared. Cold dishes consisted of salmon, deviled crab, ham, corned beef, or tongue, salads of lobster, chicken, or potato, and pickles and olives. An assortment of breads, both hot and cold, was also offered. Desserts were simple: ice cream, small cakes, and fruit. Coffee, tea, and hot chocolate accompanied dessert.

The recipes of *The Victorian Seaside Cookbook* are all authentic to the period. They have been chosen because they are delicious, interesting, and representative of the place and time. Some are old favorites, while others have well-nigh disappeared over the years. The recipes were adapted from contemporary cookbooks and painstakingly updated, using

President Grover Cleveland and family boarding a Central Railroad of New Jersey train to return to Washington, D.C. The Jersey Shore attracted other nineteenth-century Presidents and their families. President Ulysses S. Grant began summering at Long Branch in 1868. By 1876, Long Branch was known as the "summer capitol." Presidents Rutherford B. Hayes and William McKinley also visited in Long Branch. Benjamin Harrison vacationed at Cape May, and Chester A. Arthur traveled to both resorts.

modern cooking terms, techniques, measurements, and ingredients. The cookbooks of the day are a treasure-trove of information about Victorian life and attitudes. Some were authoritatively written by the outstanding chefs and cooking teachers of the day. The original style of the recipes tends to be vague on details, measurements, and cooking times. When Fanny Farmer published her *Boston Cooking School Cook Book* in 1896, she precipitated a revolution in the style of cookbook writing by introducing the detail and precision to which modern cooks are now accustomed.

Many of the cookbooks consulted include not only recipes but menus for all occasions, directions for making elaborate centerpieces, instructions for what to serve with what, and authoritative dicta on such important matters as the order in which guests should proceed to the dining room. The Victorians loved rules, and there were rules for everything: the precise distance between compotes and candelabra; exactly how many inches of tablecloth must hang from the table; and just how and with what the table must be set.

It has been said of the Victorian era that too much was never enough, and in no other aspect of life was this excess more marked than in food and its presentation. By 1902, however, one can sense the beginnings of change in the menus of the Jersey Shore hotels. They were starting to simplify. Fewer courses and dishes were being offered. Once started, the changes came quickly. Twenty years later the *White House Cookbook* was advising readers that elaborate napkin folding, so admired in the Victorian era, was déclassé. A new era had begun.

The illustrations in this book have been taken mainly from materials in the collections of the New Jersey Historical Society. The menus consulted were drawn from several collections. For their invaluable assistance in locating hotel menus, the authors wish to acknowledge Ronald J. Becker, Special Collections, Alexander Library, Rutgers University; Elaine Abrahamson, Barbara E. Koedel, and Lois MacFarland, the Atlantic County Historical Society; and Marie E. Boyd, Atlantic City Free Public Library. Valuable preliminary research was performed by Suzanne Gaby, intern, New Jersey Historical Society.

For those who would like to delve more deeply into Victorian cookery and the history of the Jersey Shore resorts, the following books are suggested.

Books on Victorian cookery:

Beeton, Isabella. *Beeton's Book of Household Management.* London: S. O. Beeton, 1861. Reprint. London: Jonathan Cape Ltd., 1968.

Farmer, Fanny. *The Boston Cooking School Cook Book.* Boston: Little Brown and Co., 1896. Reprinted as *The Original Boston Cooking School Cookbook.* New York: Weathervane Books, Crown Publishers, n.d.

Francatelli, Charles E. *The Modern Cook: Practical Guide to the Culinary Art in All Its Branches.* London: n.p., 1846. Reprint of 1880 American edition. New York: Dover Publications, 1973.

Harland, Marion [pseud.]. *Breakfast, Luncheon and Tea*. New York: Scribner, Armstrong and Co., 1875. Marion Harland was the pseudonym of novelist and writer on household affairs, Mary Virginia Hawes Terhune, mistress of Sunnybank in Pompton Lakes, New Jersey, and mother of writer Albert Payson Terhune.

The Illustrated History of American Eating and Drinking. Part 1. The American Heritage Cookbook. New York: Simon and Schuster, 1964.

Jones, Evan. *American Food: The Gastronomic Story*. New York: Vintage Books, 1974.

Local Recipes, Donated by the Ladies of Keyport, New Jersey. Keyport, N.J.: Keyport Press Print, 1891. For a full listing of later nineteenth-century charitable cookbooks published in New Jersey see: Cook, Margaret, "New Jersey's Charitable Cooks: a Checklist of Fund-Raising Cook Books Published in New Jersey (1879–1915)," *The Journal of the Rutgers University Library* 35 (December 1971): 15–26.

Parola, Maria. *Mrs. Parola's New Cook Book*. Troy, N.Y.: H. B. Nims and Co., 1882.

The Picayune's Creole Cook Book, 2d. ed. New Orleans: The Picayune, 1901. Reprint. New York: Dover Publications, 1971.

Practical Housekeeping: A Careful Compilation of Tried and Approved Recipes. Minneapolis: The Buckeye Publishing Co., 1883. Reprinted as *The Buckeye Cookbook: Traditional American Recipes*. New York: Dover Publications, 1975.

Ranhofer, Charles. *The Epicurean: A Complete Treatise of Analytical and Practical Studies of the Culinary Art*. New York: R. Ranhofer, 1893. Reprinted as *The Epicurean*. New York: Dover Publications, 1971.

Rorer, S. T. *Mrs. Rorer's Cook Book*. Philadelphia: Arnold and Co., ca. 1890.

Tschirky, Oscar. *The Cook Book by "Oscar" of the Waldorf*. New York: Werner Co., 1896. Reprinted as *"Oscar" of the Waldorf's Cookbook*. New York: Dover Publications, 1973.

Books on the history of the Jersey Shore:

Cunningham, John T. *The New Jersey Shore*. New Brunswick, N.J.: Rutgers University Press, 1958.

Funnell, Charles E. *By the Beautiful Sea*. New York: Alfred A. Knopf, 1975.

Kobbé, Gustav. *Jersey Coast and Pines*. Short Hills, N.J.: Gustav Kobbé, 1889. Reprint. Baltimore: Gateway Press, Inc., 1970.

Thomas, George E. and Doebley, Carl. *Cape May, Queen of the Seaside Resorts*. Cranbury, N.J.: Associated University Presses Inc., 1976.

Ulyat, William C. *Life at the Seashore*. Princeton, N.J.: McGinness and Runyan, 1880.

Wilson, Harold F. *The Story of the Jersey Shore*. Princeton, N.J.: D. Van Nostrand, 1964.

Haddon House, Atlantic City, 1878. "The view of the ocean from this house is uninterrupted for miles up and down the beach."

SOUPS

BEEF BOUILLON

In the Jersey Shore hotel menus of the early Victorian era, soup was presented as the first course. It was customary to offer both a clear and a thick soup. Beginning in the 1880s soups moved to the second course, appearing after the oysters and clams.

5 pounds shin beef
2 carrots, cut in pieces
2 celery ribs, cut in pieces
1 large onion, cut in pieces
10 peppercorns
2 bay leaves
1 teaspoon thyme
1/2 cup marjoram
1/4 cup parsley, chopped
2 teaspoons salt (or to taste)

Place the meat in a roasting pan and bake at 375° for 1 hour, turning occasionally to brown on all sides. Add the carrots, celery, and onion and bake 1/2 hour longer.

In a large kettle, place the meat, vegetables, and all other ingredients except the salt. Be sure to rinse and use all the glaze from the roasting pan. Cover with water to a depth of 1 inch. Cover the kettle, bring to a boil, and simmer 4 hours. Strain the broth into a large container for refrigeration. Chill and remove the cake of fat from the top. Cook the stock uncovered until it is the desired strength. Season with salt.

Yields 8 cups.

A Reading Railroad advertisement, 1897. When rail lines began to be extended to the Jersey Shore in the 1850s, rapid development followed. A trip from Philadelphia, which previously had taken two to three days by carriage, was shortened to two to three hours, and thousands of vacationers discovered the shore for the first time.

JELLIED BEEF BOUILLON

2 cups beef bouillon
1½ teaspoons gelatin
1 tablespoon marsala or medium sherry
garnish: lemon wedges

Heat the bouillon. Add the gelatin which has been softened in 2 tablespoons of water and wine. Bring to a simmer. Allow to cool overnight.

Serve mounded in wine glasses with a wedge of lemon.

Serves 4.

A hotel advertisement, 1890.

BRUNOISE

This is a sparkling, clear beef consommé with a vegetable
garnish. The vegetables are cooked separately to preserve
the clarity of the consommé.

   4 cups beef bouillon
   2 egg whites and shells, crushed
   1 cup water
   2 tablespoons butter
   1 carrot, finely diced
   1 celery rib, finely diced
   2 scallions, finely sliced into rings
   salt and black pepper (to taste)

Pour the bouillon into a large pot. Be careful not to allow
any sediment to be added. Lightly beat the egg whites with
the water and add this to the bouillon with the crushed egg
shells. Bring the stock to a boil and simmer for 1 hour. Skim
the foam from the top and strain the stock through a sieve
that has been lined with several layers of cheese cloth. You
now have a clear consommé.

Melt the butter in a small saucepan and add the finely
diced and sliced vegetables. Spoon 2 or 3 tablespoons of the
consommé over the vegetables, cover the pan, and braise
the vegetables slowly for about 10 minutes or until tender.

To serve, reheat the consommé and garnish it with the
braised vegetables. Season to taste with salt and black
pepper.

Serves 6.

MOCK TURTLE SOUP

Green turtle soup was so popular that no meal seemed complete without it. If the catch of the day did not include a large sea turtle, the chef had to improvise with ingredients at hand, and so we have mock turtle soup.

Veal Stock

3 pounds veal breast
4 ounces ham
2 carrots, coarsely chopped
2 celery ribs, coarsely chopped
1 onion, chopped
1 bay leaf
4 cloves
4 sprigs parsley
$1/2$ teaspoon thyme
1 tablespoon salt
about 12 cups water

Place all the ingredients, including about 12 cups of water, in a large kettle. Bring to a boil and simmer about 4 hours. Remove the meat and strain the broth. Chill thoroughly and remove the cake of fat that forms on the top. Remove the meat from the bones and dice. Set aside.

Veal Balls

$3/4$ pound chopped veal
1 tablespoon parsley
1 teaspoon lemon peel
1 egg
1 tablespoon flour
1 teaspoon salt
$1/4$ teaspoon black pepper
6 tablespoons butter

Combine all the ingredients except the butter. Roll into small balls and sauté in the butter until browned.

Assembling the Soup

6 tablespoons flour
butter from veal balls
1 cup cooled stock
remaining strained stock
1 cup medium sherry
1 teaspoon salt
¹/₂ teaspoon cayenne pepper
1 teaspoon Worcestershire sauce
garnish: 2 eggs, hard-cooked, sliced; 1 lemon, sliced

In a large kettle, stir the flour into the melted butter. Blend in the cooled stock and cook until it is thickened. Gradually add the remaining stock. Bring this to a boil, stirring to blend. Add the sherry, salt, cayenne, pepper and Worcestershire sauce. Add the veal pieces and veal balls. Serve in heated bowls. Garnish with sliced egg and lemon.

Serves 6.

Waiting for the train in Cape May, 1875.

OXTAIL SOUP

1½ to 2 pounds oxtail
2 tablespoons shortening
8 cups water
2 teaspoons salt
½ teaspoon black pepper
1 teaspoon sugar
1 cup carrots, sliced
1 cup onions, chopped
½ cup turnips, chopped
½ cup celery, chopped
1 bay leaf
3 drops Tabasco sauce
½ cup dry sherry
¼ cup Worcestershire sauce
¼ cup lemon juice
garnish: parsley, finely chopped (about 3 tablespoons)

In a 3-quart soup pot, brown the oxtail on all sides in hot shortening, taking care not to burn. Add the water, salt, and black pepper. Bring to a boil. Cover and reduce the heat. Simmer until the meat is tender (about 3 hours). Remove the oxtail and, when cool enough to handle, separate the meat from the bones. Skim, strain, and remove as much fat as possible from the broth. Cut the meat into bite-size pieces and return to the broth.

Add the sugar, carrots, onions, turnip, celery, and bay leaf. Bring to a boil, reduce the heat, and continue to simmer, covered, for 35 minutes.

Remove the bay leaf. Add the Tabasco sauce, sherry, Worcestershire sauce, and lemon juice. Stir and simmer a few minutes longer. Add more salt, if necessary.

Ladle into bowls and sprinkle lightly with the finely chopped parsley.

Serves 8.

CHICKEN GUMBO

Gumbo is a southern dish. Several traditionally southern dishes appear on the shore hotel menus, reflecting the popularity of these hotels with visitors from the South.

1/2 chicken, cut up
8 cups water
1 tablespoon salt
1 teaspoon black pepper
1/4 teaspoon thyme
6 tomatoes, skinned and chopped (or 2 cups canned)
1 cup onion, chopped
1 bay leaf
1/2 pound fresh okra (or 10-ounce package frozen,
    thawed) cut in crosswise slices
3 drops Tabasco sauce
2 teaspoons sugar
2 tablespoons vinegar
additional salt (if necessary)
2 cups cooked rice (optional)

Place the chicken in a 3-quart saucepan. Add the water, salt, black pepper, and thyme. Cover and bring to a boil. Turn the heat to low and simmer until very tender (about 2 hours). Remove the chicken. Skim and strain the broth and remove the excess fat. When the chicken is cool enough to handle, remove the skin and bones and cut the meat into bite-size pieces.

Return the chicken to the broth. Add the tomatoes, onions, and bay leaf. Simmer for 30 minutes.

Remove the bay leaf. Add the okra, Tabasco sauce, sugar, and vinegar. Simmer for 30 minutes (25 minutes if frozen okra is used). Add more salt, if necessary.

Divide the soup into 8 bowls and serve. If rice is used, divide the rice into 8 bowls and ladle the soup over it.

Serves 8.

CHICKEN CONSOMMÉ

1 chicken or 3 pounds chicken wings and backs
3 quarts water
1 onion
3 stalks celery
2 carrots
1 tablespoon salt
1/2 teaspoon white pepper

Place all ingredients in a large kettle and bring to a boil. Cover and reduce the heat. Let the consommé simmer for 2 1/2 hours. Skim, strain, and remove all the fat. Continue to simmer, uncovered, for another 1/2 hour to intensify flavor. Add additional salt, if necessary.

Yields 7 cups.

CONSOMMÉ À LA ROYALE

This dish and the following five consommés are all variations on the basic chicken consommé.

3 egg yolks
1/2 cup milk
1/4 teaspoon salt
cups chicken consommé, heated to the boiling point.

Combine the egg yolks, milk, and salt and beat well. Pour into a small, well-buttered baking dish. Place the dish in a larger baking pan of hot water. Bake at 350° until the custard is firm (30 to 35 minutes). Turn out on a board and when cool cut into 6 diamonds or other shapes.

Divide the consommé into 6 bowls and place one custard shape in each one. Serve at once.

Serves 6.

CONSOMMÉ COLBERT

7 cups chicken consommé
$1/2$ cup cooked celery, carrots, onion, and peas, mixed
8 eggs, poached in salted water

Add the vegetables to the consommé in a saucepan and bring to a boil. Divide into 8 bowls and place 1 poached egg in each. Serve at once.

Serves 8.

Checking-in at the West End Hotel, Long Branch, 1875. The Jersey Shore hotels were generally long, wooden structures, a few storeys high. Guests were shown "out" to their rooms, rather than "up." The West End was considered a first-class hotel. It boasted hot and cold baths, a hydraulic elevator, and rooms at $4.50 a day, with meals.

CONSOMMÉ JULIENNE

4 cups chicken consommé
$1/4$ cup each carrots and celery, cut into thin, $1^{1}/_{2}$-to-2-inch strips, cooked
$1/4$ cup onion, cut into very thin strips about 1 inch long, cooked
$1/4$ teaspoon tarragon
salt (to taste)

Place all the ingredients in a saucepan. Bring to a boil and serve.

Serves 6.

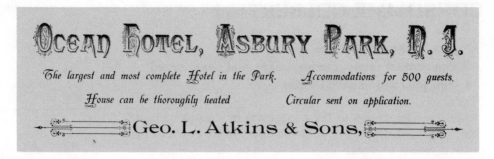

CONSOMMÉ PRINCESS

6 cups chicken consommé
³/₄ cup cooked chicken breast, diced
¹/₂ cup peas
salt (to taste)

Place the chicken and consommé into a saucepan and bring to a boil. Add the peas. Reduce the heat and cook for 3 minutes. Add salt, if necessary.
Divide into 8 bowls and serve.

Serves 8.

CONSOMMÉ AU TAPIOCA

8 cups chicken or beef consommé
1 ounce pearl tapioca
garnish: 6 small sprigs parsley

Soak the tapioca overnight. Drain and rinse. Place the consommé and the tapioca in a saucepan and bring to a boil. Reduce the heat and simmer, uncovered, for 1¹/₄ hours, stirring often.
Divide into bowls and garnish each one with a small sprig of parsley placed in the middle.

Serves 4 to 6.

CONSOMMÉ VERMICELLI

¼ cup celery, thinly sliced
5 cups chicken consommé
1 ounce vermicelli, broken into 2½-inch lengths
⅛ teaspoon cayenne pepper
salt (to taste)
Parmesan cheese, grated

Add the celery to the consommé. Simmer for 10 minutes.
Add the vermicelli and gently boil for 10 to 12 more minutes,
stirring often. Add the cayenne pepper and salt.
Divide into bowls and sprinkle with Parmesan cheese.

Serves 6 to 8.

The Mount Vernon Hotel, Cape May, 1853. This short-lived hotel
was planned on a grandiose scale to accomodate 2,100 guests,
with a bath for every room. It was to be the largest hotel in the
world and marked Cape May's hey-day as the premier Jersey
Shore resort. The hotel was never fully completed, and it burned
to the ground in 1856. Cape May's fortunes as a resort declined
after the Civil War, when patronage by southern planters fell off.

CHICKEN À LA REINE

This classic soup, chicken "to the queen's taste," has its roots deep in the Middle Ages, when ground almonds were used as the thickener instead of the rice in the recipe below. At various times through the centuries it has been thickened with egg yolks, bread crumbs, and flour as well as almonds and rice.

It was a very popular soup at the Jersey Shore hotels during this period.

3 half chicken breasts

2 stalks celery

8 cups water

1 teaspoon salt

1/2 cup cooked rice

1/4 teaspoon white pepper

1/2 cup light cream

garnish: 1 egg yolk, hard-cooked; 2 tablespoons parsley, finely chopped

Place the chicken and celery in a 3-quart saucepan. Add the water and salt and bring to a boil. Cover and reduce the heat. Simmer for 2 hours.

Remove the chicken and celery. Skim, strain, and remove the excess fat from the broth. (There should be about 2 cups.) When the chicken is cool enough to handle, remove the skin and bones.

In a blender, thoroughly blend the broth, chicken, rice, and celery. Return to the saucepan. Add the white pepper and bring to the boiling point. Blend in the cream. Add additional salt, if necessary. Divide into 6 bowls. Garnish.

To prepare the garnish, rub the egg yolk through a sieve and combine with the parsley. Divide into 6 portions and place 1 portion in each bowl.

Serves 6.

CREAM OF OYSTER SOUP

The popular New Jersey oyster sometimes found its way onto menus in the form of soup. In 1847 two New Jersey brothers, John and Adam Exeter, developed the oyster cracker. It was hailed as the perfect accompaniment to oyster soup.

2 pints oysters
1 quart half-and-half cream, or 2 cups milk and 2
    cups heavy cream
1/2 teaspoon marjoram
1 celery rib with leaves
1 teaspoon salt
1/2 teaspoon white pepper
2 tablespoons butter

Checking-in at the Ocean Hotel, Long Branch, 1872. A sojourn at the shore required considerable preparation. Guests arrived with trunks and valises of clothing for every occasion. Ulyat's 1880 guidebook to the seashore advised that guests should take a broad-brimmed hat, a bathing costume, spades and buckets, green spectacles, a spy glass, a microscope, books and games, medicines (especially for diarrhea and constipation), a lunch basket, and baseball shoes.

Heat the oysters in their own liquor until their edges begin to curl, but no longer or the oysters will toughen. Heat the cream with the marjoram and celery until it simmers. Strain it into the pan with the oysters and their liquor. Season with salt and white pepper. Heat but do not boil. Serve in hot bowls with a teaspoon of butter on each serving.

Serves 6.

CLAM BROTH

This soup is a bonus from steamed clams. It was served for breakfast as at the Seaside House in Atlantic City. It may be served cold in the summer or hot in winter with a pat of parsley butter on top.

  2 quarts clams, littleneck or steamers
  1¹/₂ cups water
  2 tablespoons butter
  celery salt
  cayenne pepper

Scrub the clams well with a brush. Place the clams in a steamer or improvise with a colander in a large kettle. Pour the water into the kettle and cover. Bring to a boil and steam the clams only until just opened, about 5 to 10 minutes.

Serve the clams in their shells with melted butter for dipping. Serve the strained soup in hot cups, topped with a pat of butter and a shake of celery salt and cayenne pepper, if desired.

Serves 4.

CLAM SOUP

  1 quart clams with liquor (fresh, frozen, or
    canned)
  4 slices bacon or salt pork, chopped
  1 large onion, sliced
  2 tablespoons flour
  3 cups water
  3 cups potatoes, cut in ³/₄-inch cubes
  1 tablespoon salt
  ¹/₂ teaspoon white pepper
  4 tablespoons butter
  4 cups hot milk

Drain the clams and reserve the liquid. Sauté the bacon in a kettle. Remove the bacon bits and sauté the onion in the bacon fat. Stir in the flour and cook to thicken. Add the water and the reserved clam liquid. Add the potatoes and cook until just tender.

If large quahog clams are used, chop the hard part of clams and add with the potatoes. Add the soft part of the clams after potatoes are tender. If using smaller clams, mince and add them when the potatoes are tender and simmer 5 minutes. Add the salt, white pepper, butter, and hot milk. Heat but do not boil. Serve with large plain crackers.

Serves 6 to 8.

~~~~~~~~~~~~~~~~~~~~~~~~~~~~~~~~~~~

CLAM CHOWDER WITH TOMATOES

6 slices bacon, chopped

2 onions

2 carrots

3 celery ribs with leaves

1 green pepper

1 28-ounce can tomatoes

1 bay leaf

1 teaspoon thyme

2 cups beef bouillon

2 large potatoes

1 quart clams with liquor (fresh, frozen, or canned)

¹/₄ cup parsley, chopped

2 teaspoons salt (or to taste)

1 teaspoon black pepper (or to taste)

Sauté the bacon in a large kettle. Dice the onions, carrots, celery, and green pepper and add to the bacon. Sauté until soft and golden but not brown. Add the tomatoes, bay leaf, thyme, and bouillon and simmer ¹/₂ hour. Peel and cube the potatoes, add them to the chowder and simmer ¹/₂ hour or until the potatoes are tender.

Chop the clams and add them with the parsley to the chowder. Simmer 5 minutes. Do not boil the chowder after the clams have been added. Season to taste with salt and black pepper.

Serves 6.

CREAM OF CAULIFLOWER SOUP

2 pounds cauliflower
1 small onion, chopped
1 celery rib, chopped
1 bay leaf
1½ cups chicken stock
1 cup light cream
½ cup heavy cream
¾ teaspoon salt (or to taste)
⅛ teaspoon white pepper (or to taste)
garnish: watercress or parsley

Separate the cauliflower into flowerets. Place them in a kettle with the onion, celery, and bay leaf. Cover with boiling water and boil 15 minutes or until it is tender. Discard the bay leaf, drain the vegetables, discard the water, and purée or mash them well.

Return the purée to the kettle. Add the chicken stock and bring to a boil. Stir in the light and heavy cream. Season to taste with salt and white pepper.

Serve in heated bowls. Garnish with a sprig of watercress or parsley. This soup may also be served chilled.

Serves 6.

TOMATO BOUILLON

Legend has it that Col. Robert Gibbon Johnson of New Jersey was instrumental in popularizing the tomato. Known and prized only by a few in colonial days, the tomato was generally thought to be toxic or an aphrodisiac. Johnson is said to have stood on the steps of the Salem County courthouse in 1820 and eaten a tomato before a large crowd, thus proving the tomato's safety. Harrison W. Crosby of Middlesex County is credited with first canning the tomato in a tin can in 1845. By 1870 the tomato was one of the most commonly available canned vegetables.

2 cups beef bouillon

3 cups tomato juice

1/2 cup green pepper, chopped

2 teaspoons lemon juice

1 teaspoon Worcestershire sauce

1 teaspoon sugar

1/2 teaspoon salt

1/8 teaspoon cloves

1/4 teaspoon black pepper

1 garlic clove

3 tablespoons sour cream

In a large saucepan, combine the bouillon and all ingredients except the garlic and sour cream. Bring to a boil and simmer 10 minutes. Strain the soup into a container for refrigeration. Peel the garlic clove, stick with a toothpick, and drop into the soup. Chill 8 hours or overnight. Remove the garlic before serving.

Serve in chilled bowls or cups. Top with a dollop of sour cream.

Serves 8.

The dining hall of the Ocean Hotel, Long Branch, 1872. The
Ocean Hotel was one of Long Branch's principal hotels. It was
conveniently located adjacent to the steamboat landing. Its enormous dining hall was the setting for theatricals and concerts in
the evening. In commenting on the virtues of the New Jersey hotel
guest in 1875, *Lippincott's Magazine* noted that "he does not tyr-
annize over and nag at the waiters nor jangle the bells as a sum-
mons to the proprietor for supposed derelictions, like an English-
man; he does not sputter and sprawl and gormandize, and
afterward haggle over the bill, like the big French vicomte; . . . he
does not wail over the quality of his wine. . . or send a dozen
waiters to collect the materials for his salad, and then some
night fold up his discontent and insolently steal away. . . ."

FISH & SEAFOOD

BROILED BLUEFISH MAÎTRE D'HÔTEL

4 bluefish fillets
salt (to taste)
melted butter

Place the bluefish fillets, skin down, on a well-greased, pre-heated broiling pan. Sprinkle with salt and brush well with melted butter. Broil the bluefish 3 to 4 inches from the heat for 6 to 10 minutes, depending on the thickness of the fillets. If the fillets are thick, they should be turned over during the broiling. Place the fillets on a warm platter and serve with butter maître d'hôtel.

Butter maître d'hôtel

1 cup soft butter
5 tablespoons lemon juice
2 tablespoons parsley, finely chopped
1 tablespoon chives, finely chopped (optional)
$1/2$ teaspoon salt (or to taste)
$1/8$ teaspoon white pepper

Cream the butter. Blend in the lemon juice, parsley, chives, salt, and white pepper. Place in a serving bowl and chill well before serving. Yields approximately 1$1/4$ cups.

Serves 4.

BOILED HADDOCK WITH EGG SAUCE

1 2½-to-3-pound haddock
1 carrot, sliced
1 onion, sliced
1 tablespoon vinegar
water, salted and boiling
garnish: lemon wedges and parsley

Tie the haddock in cheese cloth. Add the carrot, onion, and vinegar to the boiling water. Lower the fish into the salted, boiling water, reduce the heat, and simmer for about 25 minutes or until the fish flakes easily. Remove the fish gently from the water. Drain. Remove the cheese cloth and place the fish on a heated platter. Garnish with lemon wedges and parsley. Serve with egg sauce.

Egg Sauce

4 tablespoons butter
4 tablespoons flour
½ teaspoon salt (or to taste)
¼ teaspoon white pepper
1½ cups hot milk
1 teaspoon parsley, chopped
1 teaspoon chives, chopped
2 hard-cooked eggs, chopped

Melt the butter over low heat. Blend in the flour and stir the mixture until smooth and bubbly. Remove from the heat. Add the salt and white pepper and stir in the hot milk. Return to the heat, bring to a boil, reduce the heat, and cook for 8 to 9 minutes over low heat, stirring constantly.

Remove the sauce from the heat and carefully stir in the parsley, chives, and eggs. Serve with the haddock. Yields approximately 2 cups.

Serves 6.

BAKED HALIBUT WITH PORT SAUCE

2 pounds halibut steaks (scrod may be substituted)
1 medium onion
2 stalks celery
3 tablespoons butter
1/4 teaspoon each thyme, savory, salt, and white pepper
1 tablespoon butter
1 tablespoon flour
1 cup ruby port
juice of one lemon

Rinse the steaks and pat them dry. Dice the onion and celery. Melt 3 tablespoons butter in a frying pan large enough to hold the fish. Sauté the onion and celery in the butter until just wilted. Stir in the thyme, savory, salt, and white pepper. Place the fish on top of the vegetable mixture. Dot with 1 tablespoon butter. Cover (aluminum foil will do) and bake at 350° for 1/2 hour or until the fish flakes when pricked with a fork.

Remove the fish to a serving dish and keep it warm. Stir the 1 tablespoon of flour into the vegetables in the frying pan. Stir in the port and the lemon juice. Cook until thickened slightly, about 5 minutes. Add salt if necessary, and strain the sauce over the fish. The port sauce has a lovely pink color.

Serves 4 to 6.

POACHED SALMON WITH LOBSTER OR OYSTER SAUCE

2 salmon steaks
1 quart water
1 cup dry vermouth
1 celery rib with leaves
1 small onion, sliced
1 bay leaf
5 peppercorns
¼ teaspoon thyme

Wipe the steaks clean. Boil together the remaining ingredients for 5 minutes. Gently lower the salmon into the pan. Allow the water to bubble slightly at the edge. Simmer gently for 5 minutes or until the fish is cooked through. Lift the fish out with a spatula and allow it to drain before placing it on a serving plate. Serve with lobster or oyster sauce.

"Squidding" for bluefish at Asbury Park, 1880. Sport fishing was a great attraction for visitors to the shore resorts. Bluefish, striped bass, white perch, sea bass, flounder, porgie, and codfish were among the fish to be caught.

Lobster Sauce

1 tablespoon butter
1 tablespoon flour
1/2 cup poaching liquid from salmon
1/4 teaspoon salt
1/2 cup lobster meat, cooked and shredded
lobster coral, if available

Make a paste with the butter and flour. Stir it into the boiling liquid until thickened. Stir in the salt, lobster, and sieved coral. Heat to serve. Yields 1 cup.

Oyster Sauce

1 cup oysters
2 tablespoons butter
1 tablespoon flour
1 teaspoon salt
1/2 teaspoon black pepper
dash of cayenne pepper
milk, as necessary
1 tablespoon lemon juice
1 tablespoon parsley, chopped

Drain the oysters and reserve the liquid. Melt the butter in a saucepan and stir in the flour, salt, black pepper, and cayenne pepper. Cook until bubbly. Add enough milk to the oyster liquid to make one cup. Whisk the liquid into the flour mixture and bring to a boil, stirring constantly, until the sauce is slightly thickened. Stir in the oysters and cook gently until the edges of the oysters just begin to curl. Stir in the lemon juice and parsley. Yields 2 cups.

Serves 2.

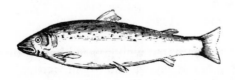

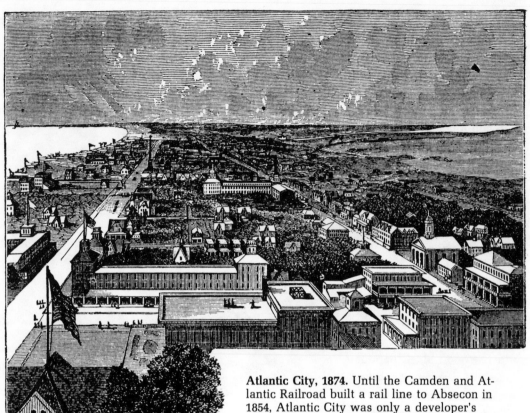

Atlantic City, 1874. Until the Camden and Atlantic Railroad built a rail line to Absecon in 1854, Atlantic City was only a developer's dream. As the town began to grow in size and reputation, doctors recommended it for its "dry, solubrious atmosphere," especially beneficial for those with rheumatic and liver complaints. By 1874 its avenues were "studded with some 600 to 700 cottages, boarding houses, hotels, and stores, each . . . vying with its neighbor for supremacy."

BAKED SEA BASS WITH SAUCE NORMANDE

1 3-pound sea bass, prepared for baking
salt and black pepper (to taste)
melted butter
garnish: lemon wedges

Place the sea bass in a well-greased baking dish. Sprinkle with salt and black pepper and brush well with the melted butter. Bake the bass at 400° for 30 minutes or until tender, basting every 10 minutes. Place the fish on a warm platter and cover with sauce normande. Garnish with lemon wedges.

Sauce normande

2 tablespoons butter

1 tablespoon flour

1 cup hot fish stock (or substitute bottled clam juice)

2 egg yolks

1/2 cup light cream

1/2 teaspoon salt

1/8 teaspoon white pepper

Melt the butter over low heat and blend in the flour. Cook until the mixture is smooth. Gradually add the fish stock (the recipe for which follows), stirring constantly. Bring to a boil, reduce the heat, and let the mixture simmer for 8 minutes, stirring often.

In a separate bowl, beat the egg yolks. Add the hot fish stock mixture a little at a time, beating constantly. Add the cream and return the sauce to the heat. Stir in the salt and white pepper. Bring almost to a boil (no higher than 175°) and cook for 1 minute, stirring constantly. Serve with the sea bass. Yields 1 cup.

Fish Stock

1/2 pound fish bones and trimmings

1 onion, sliced

2 tablespoons parsley, chopped

2 tablespoons lemon juice

1/2 teaspoon salt

1 1/2 cups water

1/2 cup dry white wine

Place all the ingredients in a pot. Bring to a boil over high heat. Reduce the heat and continue to boil lightly for 30 minutes, skimming off the residue that rises to the surface. Strain the stock through a fine sieve. The leftover stock may be frozen. Yields 1 to 1 1/2 cups.

Serves 4.

OYSTERS ON THE HALF-SHELL

When the early colonists came to America they found huge quantities of oysters that were far larger and more delicious than any they had known in England. The oyster became an important food along the Atlantic coast. In the nineteenth century the enthusiasm for oysters bordered on becoming a national obsession. Oysters could be packed in ice and shipped by rail and steamship to inland cities and small towns. By 1880, even though some of the old sources were near depletion, the demand for oysters remained unabated. Visitors to the Jersey Shore were no less enthusiastic than other Americans, and the oyster industry at Keyport and Barnegat Bay was thriving. "Diamond Jim" Brady, a frequent visitor to Long Branch, was said to consume two to three dozen oysters three times a day.

24 or 32 oysters (depending on size)
4 plates crushed ice
black pepper
1 lemon, quartered

When buying fresh oysters in the shell, make sure the oysters are alive, with tightly closed shells. Use them the same day they are purchased.

Scrub the oyster shells thoroughly and rinse well in cold water. Open each oyster carefully by inserting the point of a sharp, thin knife blade into the hinged end of the oyster and pushing forward until it cuts the muscle that holds the valves together. Run the knife around the shell. Lift off the top thinner valve. Cut the muscle that is attached to the deep half of the shell. This will leave the oyster loose in the shell. Examine the oysters for bits of shell and remove any.

Arrange 6 or 8 oysters on the half-shell on each plate of crushed ice. Sprinkle each oyster very lightly with black pepper and serve with a lemon quarter.

Serves 4.

SCALLOPED OYSTERS

The popularity of oysters assured that they appeared on almost every menu in some form. Scalloped oysters were suggested as an intermediate course between the fish and meat.

1 quart oysters, drained, with liquor reserved
1 cup dry bread crumbs
3 tablespoons butter
1 teaspoon salt
1/2 teaspoon black pepper
2 tablespoons parsley, finely chopped
1 teaspoon lemon rind, grated
1 cup light cream
paprika

Place one layer of oysters in a 2-quart baking dish. Sprinkle with part of the bread crumbs, dots of butter, salt, black pepper, parsley, and lemon rind. Continue the layers, ending with bread crumbs. Pour the reserved oyster liquor and the cream over the top layer. Dust the top lightly with paprika.
Bake at 350° for 45 to 50 minutes.

Serves 6 to 8.

CLAM FRITTERS

Clam fritters were served for breakfast at some of the Jersey Shore hotels.

   1 pint clams (fresh or canned)
   2 eggs
   1 cup milk
   1 teaspoon salt
   ¹/₂ teaspoon black pepper
   2¹/₂ cups flour
   1 tablespoon salad oil
   oil for frying

   Drain and chop the clams. The liquid may be frozen and saved for clam chowder. Beat the eggs until light and stir in the milk, salt, and black pepper. Place the flour in a bowl, add half the milk mixture, and beat until light and smooth. Add the remaining milk mixture and the oil. Stir in the clams. Drop by teaspoons into the hot oil in a skillet. Brown to a golden hue on both sides.

   Serves 4 to 6.

A crabbing party.

SOFT-SHELL CRABS WITH CRESSON SAUCE

4 soft-shell crabs, cleaned
$1/2$ cup flour
2 eggs
2 tablespoons oil
2 cups fresh bread crumbs
2 tablespoons parsley, chopped
$1/4$ teaspoon each salt and black pepper
butter and oil for sautéing
garnish: lemon wedges

Wash the crabs and pat them dry. Dredge them in the flour. Stir the eggs with the 2 tablespoons of oil in a shallow dish. Mix the bread crumbs, parsley, and seasonings in a shallow dish. Dip the dredged crabs in the eggs, then in the crumbs. Chill for $1/2$ hour.

Combine equal parts butter and oil in a frying pan to the depth of $1/4$ inch. Heat the oil and sauté the crabs on each side until golden and cooked through. Do not overcook. Garnish with lemon wedges or serve with cresson sauce.

Cresson Sauce

1 cup mayonnaise
$1/2$ cup watercress, chopped
1 tablespoon capers
1 teaspoon lemon juice

Stir together the mayonnaise, watercress, capers, and lemon juice. Serve with fried soft-shell crabs or any broiled or fried fish. Yields $1^{1}/4$ cups.

Serves 2 to 4.

LOBSTER CUTLETS WITH ANCHOVY SAUCE

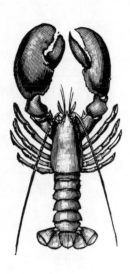

4 tablespoons butter
4 tablespoons flour
1/2 teaspoon salt
1/4 teaspoon white pepper
1 cup half-and-half cream
1 tablespoon Worcestershire sauce
1/8 teaspoon cayenne pepper
1 tablespoon lemon juice
1 cup lobster meat (fresh-cooked or canned)
1 egg
1 tablespoon oil
1 cup bread or cracker crumbs
1/4 teaspoon each salt and black pepper
1/4 cup flour
oil for sautéing
garnish: parsley

Melt the butter in a saucepan. Stir in 4 tablespoons of flour and cook until it bubbles. Stir in the salt and white pepper. Slowly add the cream, stirring constantly until the sauce is very thick. Add the Worcestershire sauce, cayenne pepper, lemon juice, and lobster meat. Pour the mixture into a greased 8x8-inch pan and chill.

Mix the egg with 1 tablespoon of oil in a shallow dish. Combine the crumbs and seasonings in a shallow dish. Spread the flour in another shallow dish. Form the well-chilled lobster mixture into 8 patties or cutlets. Roll them in the flour, then dip them in the egg and crumbs. Chill the cutlets for 1/2 hour or until ready to cook.

Sauté the cutlets in hot oil until they are golden. Serve them on a heated platter, covered with anchovy sauce. Garnish with parsley.

Anchovy Sauce

2 tablespoons butter
4 anchovy fillets
2 tablespoons cream

Melt the butter in a saucepan and mash the anchovy fillets in the butter. Stir in the cream, and heat. Serve with lobster cutlets. Yields approximately 1/3 cup.

Serves 4.

An advertisement for the Clarence House, Barnegat, 1881. It boasts of seafood from Barnegat Bay and facilities for sport fishing.

LOBSTER SALAD

2 cups lobster meat (fresh-cooked or canned)
2 tablespoons lemon juice
3 tablespoons salad oil
1/2 teaspoon salt
1/4 teaspoon black pepper
2 cups celery, diced
1/4 cup scallions, diced
1 cup mayonnaise
lettuce
garnish: shelled claws, hard-cooked eggs,
    olives, or capers

Dice the lobster meat. Claw meat may be kept whole to use as a garnish. (Extra claws may be purchased in your local fish market.) Mix together the lemon juice, salt, and black pepper. Toss with the lobster meat and allow to marinate for at least 1/2 hour. Combine the remaining ingredients and serve in lettuce cups or on a bed of shredded lettuce.

Garnish with shelled claws, hard-cooked eggs, olives, or capers.

Serves 4 to 6.

Promenading at the Jersey Shore. Promenading was a popular passtime for seashore guests, whether at Cape May (*above*) or on the Atlantic City boardwalk (*below*). The epitome of promenading was Atlantic City's Easter parade, instituted in 1876 to draw day-trippers from the United States Centennial Exposition in Philadelphia. In the 1880s saltwater taffy became a popular item sold on the boardwalk.

POULTRY

CHICKEN WITH CURRY-RAISIN SAUCE

This dish was served at the Wiltshire Hotel in Atlantic City as "fricassee of chicken à la Turque."

  1 frying chicken, cut into serving pieces
  1 teaspoon salt (or to taste)
  1/3 cup shortening for frying
  3 cups chicken broth
  1/4 cup onion, finely chopped
  2 tablespoons sugar
  1 tablespoon curry powder
  1/4 teaspoon each black pepper, ginger, mace,
     thyme, and saffron
  1/8 teaspoon cayenne pepper
  2 tablespoons lemon juice
  1/4 cup butter
  1/4 cup flour
  1/3 cup golden raisins, soaked overnight in dry sherry
  2 cups cooked rice

Sprinkle the chicken with 1/4 teaspoon of the salt. Melt the shortening in a frying pan. Fry the chicken pieces over medium heat until golden brown. Remove the chicken. Pour off the fat and wipe out the frying pan. Return the chicken to the frying pan. Add the broth, the remaining 3/4 teaspoon of salt, onion, sugar, spices, and lemon juice. Bring to a boil.

Cover and reduce the heat. Simmer for 30 minutes or until the chicken is tender. Remove the chicken from the pan and keep warm. Reserve the cooking liquid.

In a saucepan, melt the butter and blend in the flour. Cook over low heat, stirring constantly, until the mixture is smooth and bubbling. Remove from the heat and slowly add the cooking liquid. Return to the heat. Add more salt, if necessary. Add the drained raisins. Simmer for 10 minutes, stirring frequently.

Arrange the chicken on a serving dish. Pour the curry sauce over it. Serve with the rice.

Serves 4.

~~~~~~

CHICKEN MARENGO

Chicken Marengo was invented by Napoleon's cook to celebrate the French victory over the Austrians at the Battle of Marengo, June 14, 1800. It is said that the cook, running short of supplies, used every food he could gather from the countryside. This American Victorian version uses tomatoes and omits the crawfish, fried eggs, olives, and fried bread used in the original recipe.

1 frying chicken, cut into serving pieces
1 teaspoon salt (or to taste)
¼ cup vegetable oil for frying
2 cups chicken broth (or water)
⅔ cup canned tomatoes
1 clove garlic, peeled
16 small white onions, peeled and boiled for 5 minutes
1 cup button mushrooms, ready for cooking
¼ teaspoon each thyme and black pepper
⅛ teaspoon cayenne pepper
½ cup dry white wine
¼ cup butter
¼ cup flour
garnish: 2 tablespoons parsley, chopped

Sprinkle the chicken with 1/4 teaspoon of the salt. Heat the oil in a frying pan over medium heat. Fry the chicken pieces until golden brown. Remove the chicken. Pour off the oil and wipe out the frying pan.

Return the chicken to the frying pan and add the broth. Put the tomatoes through a sieve to remove the seeds and add the tomatoes to the broth. Add the garlic, onions, mushrooms, thyme, black pepper, cayenne pepper, and remaining salt. Bring to a boil. Cover and reduce the heat. Simmer for 30 minutes or until the chicken is tender. Remove the chicken from the sauce. Add the white wine to the sauce, stir, and simmer for 3 minutes. Remove the garlic clove.

In a saucepan melt the butter and blend in the flour. Cook over low heat, stirring constantly, until the mixture is smooth and bubbling. Remove from the heat and slowly add the sauce. Over low heat, stir the sauce until it starts to thicken. Simmer for 10 minutes, stirring frequently. Add more salt, if necessary.

Arrange the chicken on a serving dish. Pour the sauce over it and garnish with the chopped parsley.

Serves 4.

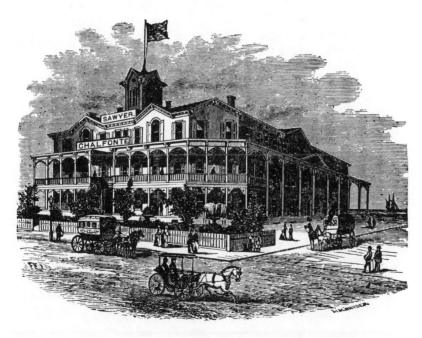

Sawyer's Chalfonte Hotel, Cape May, around 1880. The Chalfonte was built in 1875 as a medium-sized boarding house, but over the years numerous extensions were added.

RISSOLÉ OF CHICKEN

⅓ cup cooked chicken, finely chopped
2 tablespoons mushrooms, cooked, finely chopped
2 tablespoons pickled tongue (or ham), cooked and
   finely chopped
2 tablespoons thick white sauce
dash of cayenne pepper
⅛ teaspoon salt (or to taste)
1 sheet puff pastry (commercial frozen variety is
   excellent)

Mix the first 5 ingredients. Taste for salt and add, if necessary. Mix well.

Roll the puff pastry into a 13x13-inch square. Cut 16 3-inch circles with a biscuit cutter. Place ½ tablespoon of the chicken mixture into the center of each circle. Spread a few drops of water around the edge of each circle and fold the pastry circle over the chicken as for a turnover. Squeeze the edges of each semi-circle together, making a scalloped edge.

At this point the Victorian cook would have dipped the semi-circles into beaten egg, rolled them in bread crumbs, and fried them. They were served warm on a folded napkin as an entrée. Despite the Victorian love of fried foods, today's cook will prefer the taste of baked rissolé of chicken. Bake at 350° for 15 minutes or until golden brown.

Thick White Sauce

3 tablespoons butter
3 tablespoons flour
1 cup milk
¼ teaspoon salt

In a small saucepan, melt the butter and blend in the flour. Cook over low heat, stirring constantly, until the mixture is smooth. Remove from the heat and slowly pour in the milk, stirring constantly until smooth. Return to the heat. Add the salt and cook over low heat, stirring constantly, for 10 minutes. Yields 1 cup.

Serves 4.

QUENELLES

Quenelles, or little dumplings, were considered a difficult dish to prepare because the meat had to be pounded in a mortar to achieve the smooth paste. Today they are easily made in a food processor. Quenelles were served with consommé at the Hotel Albion in Atlantic City in the 1890s. They may also be served with an herb-flavored cream sauce.

1 pound veal, boneless chicken breast, or non-oily fish
1/4 teaspoon salt
1/8 teaspoon each white pepper and nutmeg
dash of cayenne pepper
1 large egg yolk
1 1/2 cups heavy cream

Trim all the fat from the meat, chill well, and cut into cubes. Place the chilled meat or fish and the seasonings into the container of a food processor. Mix in the egg yolk among the cubes of meat so it will not spatter on the sides of container. Process this mixture until smooth. Gradually add the heavy cream as the mixture is processing. Scrape the processor bowl sides and process 1/2 minute longer. Chill at least 30 minutes.

Butter the sides and bottom of a shallow, flame-proof cooking utensil. Shape the quenelles with 2 soup spoons that have been dipped in hot water. Heap the mixture high in one spoon. Dip the second spoon and press both together to make the traditional egg shape. Carefully lay the quenelle in the buttered pan. When all are shaped, carefully pour boiling water to barely cover the quenelles. Add 1/2 teaspoon salt to the water. Cover the quenelles with waxed paper that has been cut to fit and buttered. Poach for 4 minutes. Lift the paper and gently turn the quenelles. Replace the paper and continue cooking 5 minutes. Drain on paper towels.

Yields 24 to 32 quenelles.

Victorian table napkins. Elaborately folded table napkins were a favorite with Victorian era diners.

CHICKEN LIVER WITH MADEIRA SAUCE

12 chicken livers
1/2 cup flour
1 teaspoon salt
1/2 teaspoon black pepper
3 tablespoons butter
2 tablespoons salad oil
1 cup Madeira sauce (recipe page 84)

Halve the chicken livers and remove the excess fat. Dust them with the combined flour and seasonings. Heat the butter and oil together in a skillet and sauté the livers until browned but still pink in the center. Serve with Madeira sauce.

Serves 3 to 4.

BOILED FOWL WITH SAUCE SUPRÊME

A fowl is a hen more than a year old. It generally weighs 3 to 5 pounds. Victorian cookbooks are filled with advice on determining the age of a chicken since often it was chosen "on foot."

1 3-to-4-pound fowl, cut into serving pieces
water to cover
1 1/2 teaspoons salt (or to taste)
1/4 teaspoon each basil and white pepper
1 carrot
2 onions
1 celery stalk
garnish: 2 tablespoons parsley, chopped

In a large saucepan or skillet, arrange the fowl and cover with water. Add the salt, basil, white pepper, carrot, onions, and celery. Add more water to cover the vegetables. Bring quickly to a boil. Cover and reduce the heat. Simmer for 2 1/2 hours or until tender.

Lift out the pieces of fowl and remove the skin and loose bones, if you wish. Strain the broth and remove the fat. If you have less than 1½ cups of broth, add water to make that amount. Reserve the broth for sauce suprême. Arrange the fowl on a warm serving platter and pour sauce suprême over it. Sprinkle with the chopped parsley.

Sauce suprême

5 tablespoons butter
5 tablespoons flour
1½ cups broth (from cooking the fowl)
⅓ cup sauterne (or equivalent white wine)
⅔ cup light cream
salt (to taste)

In a saucepan, melt the butter and blend in the flour. Cook over low heat, stirring constantly, until the mixture is smooth and bubbling. Remove from the heat and slowly add the chicken broth, stirring until smooth. Return to the heat and simmer for 5 minutes, stirring frequently. Add the sauterne and simmer for 5 more minutes. Remove the sauce from the heat and add the cream. Stir well. Add salt, if necessary. If the sauce is not warm enough, return it to the heat briefly, stirring constantly. Do not boil. Yields approximately 2½ cups.

Serves 4 to 6.

SALMIS OF DUCK WITH OLIVES

1 4¹/₂-to-5-pound duck
2 slices bacon
1 onion, chopped
1 carrot, chopped
2 tablespoons butter
1 tablespoon oil
5 peppercorns
1 bay leaf
1 cup water
¹/₂ cup dry sherry
1 teaspoon lemon juice
12 green olives, pitted
salt and black pepper (to taste)

Remove the giblets and the neck from the duck and reserve. Remove any excess fat. Place the duck in a roasting pan and place the bacon over the breast. Roast at 400° for ³/₄ hour.

Sauté the giblets, neck, onion, and carrot in the butter and oil. When browned, add the peppercorns, bay leaf, and water. Simmer for 1¹/₂ hours and strain.

Remove the duck from the oven and cool slightly. Cut into four parts. Place in a stewing pan with the strained duck stock and any juices from the cut-up duck. Add the dry sherry and lemon juice. Simmer 30 minutes or until the duck is tender. Add the olives and heat. Season to taste with salt and black pepper.

Serves 4.

SPRING DUCK WITH APPLE SAUCE

2 4-pound ducks, split
salt (to taste)
paprika (to taste)
1 tablespoon oil
1 carrot, chopped
1 onion, chopped
3 peppercorns
1 bay leaf
1/4 teaspoon thyme
2 sprigs parsley

Remove the excess fat and any pin feathers from the ducks. Sprinkle them inside with salt and place on a rack in a roasting pan, skin side up. Dust with paprika. Prick the ducks with a fork to allow the fat to run off. Roast the ducks at 325° for 2 hours until crisp and tender.

In a saucepan, heat the oil and add the duck giblets, the neck, carrot, and onion. Brown well. Add the remaining herbs and water to cover. Simmer 1½ hours until tender. Strain and remove the fat from the stock. There should be 2 cups of stock. Place the ducks on a heated platter and keep warm until served. Serve with apple sauce.

Apple Sauce for Duck

1/4 cup wine vinegar
3 tablespoons sugar
2 cups duck stock
1 teaspoon lemon juice
2 tablespoons cornstarch
3 tablespoons ruby port or medium sherry
1 cup apple sauce

In a small saucepan, boil the vinegar with the sugar until it becomes a syrup. Gradually add the duck stock and lemon juice. Dissolve the cornstarch in the wine and add to the sauce. Cook, stirring constantly, until thickened. Stir in the apple sauce. The drippings in the duck roasting pan may be deglazed with ½ cup wine or water, strained, and added to the sauce. Yields 3 cups.

Serves 4.

ROAST SQUAB MAÎTRE D'HÔTEL

A squab is a young pigeon, not more than 4 weeks old. It was a favorite food during the Victorian era. *The Picayune's Creole Cook Book* says, "squabs are most welcome at the most recherché feast." And according to Fanny Farmer, "squabs make a delicious tidbit for the convalescent, and are often the first meat allowed a patient by the physician."

4 1-pound squabs

1/2 or 1 teaspoon salt

1 1/3 cup stuffing (or cooked, seasoned rice)

1/2 cup butter, softened

1 cup hot water

3/4 cup butter maître d'hôtel (recipe page 27)

4 pieces toast, crusts removed

garnish: 8 small bunches green grapes (3 to 5
   grapes in a bunch) and parsley

Rinse each squab inside and out and pat dry with a paper towel. Rub the inside of each squab with 1/8 or 1/4 teaspoon of salt, depending on your taste. Lightly stuff the squabs with 1/3 cup of the stuffing, using the recipe that follows (or substitute rice), and sew up the openings. Place the squabs on a rack in a shallow roasting pan. Rub the breast and legs of each squab with 2 tablespoons of the softened butter. Pour the water into the roasting pan and bake at 350° for 1 1/4 hours or until the legs easily move. For the first hour of roasting, baste every 10 minutes with the water and drippings from the bottom of the pan.

Pour out the water and drippings from the roasting pan 15 minutes before the squabs have finished roasting. Cover each squab with butter maître d'hôtel. Return to the oven for 10 minutes. Then baste once more with the butter maître d'hôtel from the bottom of the roasting pan. Bake for 5 more minutes. Remove the squab and remove the thread from the sewed-up openings.

On a warm serving platter, arrange the toast. Top each slice with a squab. Arrange the bunches of grapes and parsley around the squabs.

Lily Langtry (1852–1929). The British actress known as the "Jersey Lily," in honor of her birth on the Isle of Jersey, visited Long Branch during her tours of the United States in the late nineteenth century. The glitter and high living of Long Branch attracted many public celebrities, such as "Diamond Jim" Brady, Lillian Russell, Jay Gould, and "Boss" Tweed.

Stuffing for Squab

2 tablespoons butter
1/4 cup onion, chopped
1 1/2 cups bread crumbs
1/4 cup water
1/4 teaspoon each sage, thyme, salt, and black pepper
3 tablespoons golden raisins

In a small frying pan, melt the butter and fry the onions over low heat, stirring frequently, until the onions are limp and golden but not brown. Mix in the bread crumbs, water, sage, thyme, salt, and black pepper. Pour the butter and onions over the bread crumbs. Add the raisins and mix well. Yields 1 1/3 cups.

Serves 4.

SQUAB BORDELAISE

Reed birds bordelaise was a popular Jersey Shore dish in the 1880s. But since the tiny reed bird is not available today, squab has been substituted.

6 1-pound squabs
3 tablespoons butter
1 teaspoon each salt and paprika

Place the squabs on a broiler rack 4 inches from the flame. Combine the butter, salt, and paprika. Brush the squabs generously with the butter. Broil for 8 to 10 minutes. Turn and brush again. Broil 10 to 15 minutes, or until tender. Do not overcook. The birds may also be roasted at 375° for 30 to 35 minutes. Serve with sauce bordelaise.

Sauce bordelaise

3 tablespoons scallions, chopped
1 clove garlic, minced
2 tablespoons butter
1 cup each red wine and beef stock
2 tablespoons tomato paste
1 tablespoon cornstarch
salt and black pepper (to taste)
1 teaspoon lemon juice
1 teaspoon parsley, chopped

Sauté the scallions and garlic in the butter until softened. Add the wine and beef stock and boil to reduce to 1¹/₂ cups. Stir in the tomato paste. Dissolve the cornstarch in a small amount of water and add to the sauce, stirring constantly. Cook until slightly thickened. Add salt and black pepper to taste, and stir in the lemon juice and parsley. Yields 2 cups.

Serves 6.

PARLOR & BALLROOM.

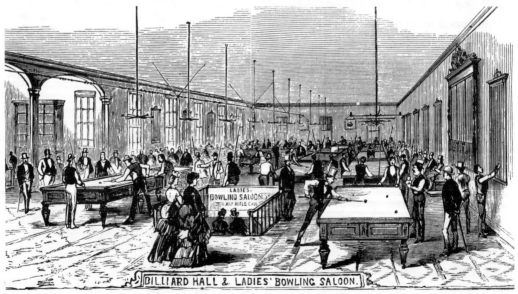

BILLIARD HALL & LADIES' BOWLING SALOON.

Scenes from the Ocean Hotel, Long Branch, 1872.

MEATS

TENDERLOIN OF BEEF À LA JARDINIERE

1 5-pound tenderloin of beef
2 cups each small carrots and pearl onions
beef broth
1 teaspoon sugar
salt (to taste)
1 tablespoon butter
1 cup each peas, Brussels sprouts, flowerets of
   cauliflower, whole green beans, and asparagus
   tips, cooked but crisp, salted to taste
1/2 cup seedless raisins, plumped in boiling water
   (optional)

Roast a 5-pound tenderloin of beef as for tenderloin of beef with bordelaise (recipe page 56).

In a saucepan, simmer the carrots and onions in the beef broth, sugar, salt, and butter until they are tender.

Place the tenderloin in the center of a large, warmed platter. Drain the vegetables and raisins (if used) and arrange them in small mounds around the roast, alternating for color and shape.

Serves 8 to 10.

TENDERLOIN OF BEEF WITH SAUCE BORDELAISE

The development of the refrigerated railroad car in the 1880s made it possible for the Jersey Shore hotels, as well as the rest of the country, to serve top-quality beef throughout the year. The tenderloin cut of beef is most often served rare.

1 5-pound tenderloin of beef
salt and black pepper (to taste)
2 layers of beef suet

Lightly dust the tenderloin with salt and black pepper. Place it on a rack with a layer of suet underneath and one on top of the roast. Put the rack in a shallow roasting pan and roast at 425°, 50 minutes for rare and 60 minutes for medium. Remove the roast to a warmed serving platter. Let it stand for 10 to 15 minutes before carving. Slice and serve with sauce bordelaise.

Sauce bordelaise

Charles Francatelli, chef to Queen Victoria, wrote in *The Modern Cook,* (1846), "This sauce must be kept rather thin, and to be perfect, should be bright and wholly free from grease."

2 cups beef broth
2 cups dry red wine
1 carrot, sliced
1 small onion
1 stalk celery
1 bay leaf
1 whole clove
1/2 teaspoon garlic powder
1/2 teaspoon black pepper
1 teaspoon salt
1/4 teaspoon thyme
1/4 teaspoon cayenne pepper
1 tablespoon plus 1 1/2 teaspoons butter
1 tablespoon plus 1 1/2 teaspoons flour

In a saucepan, place all the ingredients except the butter and flour. Bring to a boil and continue to cook over low heat, uncovered, for 40 minutes. Strain. If you have more than 1½ cups of liquid, return the liquid to the saucepan and continue to boil until it has been reduced to that amount. If you have less than 1½ cups, add enough red wine to make that amount.

In a saucepan, melt the butter over low heat. Blend in the flour and stir until it starts to bubble. Remove it from the heat and add the liquid, stirring constantly to keep it from lumping. Return the sauce to the stove and cook over low heat, stirring constantly, until the sauce is smooth and thickened. Add more salt, if necessary. Simmer and stir for 10 minutes. Yields 1½ cups.

Serves 8.

President Ulysses S. Grant and his family surf bathing at Long Branch, 1869.

PORTERHOUSE STEAK WITH ONIONS

There are few foods more American than porterhouse steak, and even fewer that have been more temptingly eulogized: Mark Twain wrote of "a mighty porter-house steak an inch and a half thick, hot and sputtering from the griddle; dusted with fragrant pepper; enriched with little melting bits of butter." Like Mark Twain, most Americans in the Victorian era preferred their steaks fried. However, some cookbooks of the time warned against frying. *The Buckeye Cookbook* (1883) urged that frying be "banished from all civilized kitchens." Broiling, on the other hand, received much praise: "Broiling is the most wholesome method of cooking meat, and is most acceptable to invalids."

1 1½-inch thick porterhouse steak
2 tablespoons shortening (for frying)
1 tablespoon butter
salt and black pepper (to taste)
fried onions

To pan fry, score the fat around the steak to keep it from curling during cooking. In a large, heavy skillet, melt the shortening. Allow it to get very hot, but not smoking. Drop the steak into the hot fat and fry for 6 minutes on each side. Place the steak on a platter and spread it with the butter. Dust with salt and black pepper. Serve with onions.

Steak prepared in this way will be rare. If you prefer your steak medium or well done, prepare it by broiling.

In preparation for broiling, preheat the broiler for 10 minutes. Score the fat around the steak. Place the steak 3 inches from the heat and broil (8 minutes on each side for rare steak, 10 minutes for medium, 12 minutes for well done). When the steak is done, place it on a platter, dot it with butter, and dust with salt and black pepper. Serve with onions.

Fried Onions

¼ cup butter
3 large onions, peeled, thinly sliced
¼ teaspoon salt
⅛ teaspoon black pepper

Melt the butter in a frying pan. Add the onions and sprinkle them with salt and black pepper. Sauté over low heat until the onions are golden brown.

Serves 2.

STANDING RIB ROAST OF BEEF WITH YORKSHIRE PUDDING

In the cookbooks and other writings of the latter half of the nineteenth century, it was common to lament the passing of the open fire for the roasting of meat. *The Buckeye Cookbook* (1883) reminds readers that, in a stove, meats are "baked, a most inferior process." If readers must use a stove, however, they were advised to place "two or three bits of wood laid cross-wise" in a roasting pan and put the standing rib roast on top of them. This was to keep the meat from resting in the water that was to be placed in the bottom of the pan.

1 6-to-8-pound standing rib roast of beef
salt and black pepper

Place the roast in a shallow roasting pan with the bone down and the fat side up. Rub the fat with salt and black pepper. For best results, insert a meat thermometer into the center of the roast, making sure it does not touch a bone. Do not cover or add water. Roast at 325° until the thermometer registers 140° for rare, 160° for medium, or 170° for well done. If you do not use a thermometer, roast the meat 25 minutes per pound for rare, 30 minutes per pound for medium, or 35 minutes per pound for well done.

Place the roast on a warmed serving platter and let it rest for 15 minutes before carving.

Yorkshire Pudding

½ cup beef drippings
3 eggs
1½ cups milk
½ teaspoon salt
1½ cups flour

In a shallow 2-quart baking pan, pour the beef drippings. Heat the pan in the oven until it is sizzling hot but not smoking.

In a mixing bowl, whisk the eggs until light. Add the milk and salt. Whisk again. Add the flour a little at a time, whisking between additions. Whisk vigorously until the batter is smooth (about 2 minutes). Pour the batter into the hot baking pan and bake at 450° for 10 minutes. Reduce the heat to 350° and bake for 15 minutes longer. Remove from the oven and cut into 8 pieces.

Serves 8.

CORNED BEEF

Corned beef appeared often on the menus of the Jersey Shore hotels and was served both cold and hot (with cabbage).

1 3-pound corned brisket of beef
1 onion, sliced
1 tablespoon vinegar
1/2 teaspoon black pepper
3 celery stalk tops

Cover the corned beef with water and let it soak for 1 to 2 hours. Rinse well. Place the beef in a large pot with other ingredients and cover with cold water. Bring the water to a boil, reduce the heat, cover, and let simmer for 3 hours.

Cold Corned Beef

1 3-pound corned beef, prepared as above
garnish: parsley or celery tops

Allow the corned beef to cool in the cooking water. Remove the beef from the cooking water, drain, and chill. Thinly slice the beef and arrange on the serving plate. Garnish with the parsley or celery tops. Serve with mustard and a variety of pickles.

Corned Beef and Cabbage

1 3-pound corned beef, prepared as above
2 small cabbages, cored and quartered
8 boiled potatoes, warmed
garnish: 2 tablespoons parsley, finely chopped

In the last 20 minutes of cooking the corned beef, add the cabbage. When the cabbage is tender, remove the beef and the cabbage and drain. (You may need to cook the cabbage 5 to 10 minutes longer than the beef.) Place the beef on a serving plate and arrange the cabbage and potatoes around it. Garnish the potatoes with the chopped parsley and serve.

Serves 8.

RAGOÛT OF BEEF PARISIENNE

A ragout is a stew made of meat or fish with or without vegetables.

3 whole tomatoes, fresh or canned
2 onions, peeled and quartered
1/8 pound fat bacon (if beef is very lean)
1/4 teaspoon cloves
1/4 teaspoon cinnamon
1/2 teaspoon black pepper
1 2 1/2-to-3-pound chuck or rump roast
1 cup water
1/4 cup vinegar
1 1/4 teaspoons salt
4 tablespoons fat from the pot (or 4 tablespoons of
   butter)
4 tablespoons flour
1 1/4 cups liquid from the pot (or a mixture of liquid
   and red wine)
1/4 cup red wine
1 cup mushrooms, sliced and sautéed

In a Dutch oven, place the tomatoes, onions, fat bacon (if used), and spices. Cut the beef into squares. Place it on top of the other ingredients in the Dutch oven. Pour in the water and vinegar. Cover tightly and bake at 325° for about 3 hours or until very tender. Check occasionally. After 2 hours, add the salt. When the meat is tender, remove it from the liquid and place it on a serving platter.

Strain the liquid in the Dutch oven and remove as much fat as possible. Reserve 1 1/4 cups of liquid. Any leftover liquid can be saved for another occasion. If there is not enough liquid, add red wine to make 1 1/4 cups.

Make a roux of the 4 tablespoons of the fat removed from the liquid (or use 4 tablespoons of butter) and the flour. Gradually stir in the liquid and cook over low heat until smooth and thickened. Add the wine. Stir and simmer for a few minutes. Add more salt, if necessary. Add the mushrooms and stir. Pour the sauce over the meat and serve.

Serves 6 to 8.

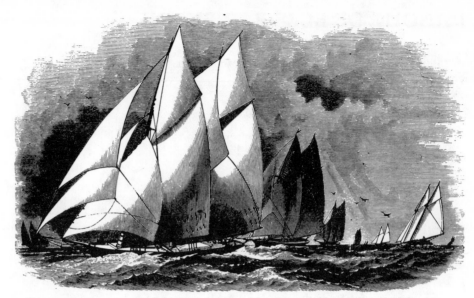

Yachting at Cape May,
1895.

BOILED BEEF

Boiled beef was often served at the Jersey Shore hotels in
early Victorian times, suggesting that the available beef was
of poorer quality.

> 1 3-pound chuck roast, with some fat
> boiling water
> ¹/₄ teaspoon red pepper flakes
> 1¹/₂ teaspoons salt

Place the roast in a Dutch oven. Cover the roast with the
boiling water and boil over high heat for 3 minutes. Reduce
the heat, add the red pepper flakes, cover, and let it simmer
for 2 hours or until the meat is very tender. After 1¹/₂ hours
add the salt. Serve the beef hot with gravy, or cold, thinly
sliced with mustard.

Gravy for Boiled Beef

4 tablespoons fat
4 tablespoons flour
1½ cups beef broth
2 tablespoons vinegar
1 teaspoon sugar
1 teaspoon salt
¼ teaspoon black pepper

Make a roux of the fat and the flour. Add the beef broth. Cook over medium heat and stir until smooth and thickened. Add the vinegar, sugar, salt, and black pepper. Stir and cook for a few more minutes. Serve over the boiled beef. Yields 1½ cups.

Mustard

¼ cup brown sugar
2 tablespoons flour
1 tablespoon dry mustard
¼ teaspoon salt
¼ teaspoon tarragon
½ cup cider vinegar

In the top of a double boiler mix the sugar, flour, mustard, salt, and tarragon. Add the vinegar, a little at a time, and stir until smooth. Place over boiling water. Cook, stirring frequently, until the mustard is thick. Cool and refrigerate. Yields ½ cup.

Serves 6 to 8.

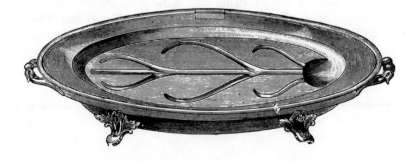

BEEF TONGUE

1 3-pound beef tongue, smoked
1 onion
1/2 teaspoon dry red peppers
1 teaspoon black pepper
6 whole cloves

Soak the tongue in water to cover overnight. The next day remove the tongue from the soaking water and rinse well. Put the tongue in a large saucepan and cover it with cold water. Add the remaining ingredients. Bring the water to a boil, reduce the heat, cover, and let it simmer for 1 hour per pound of tongue (or until the tongue is very tender). Let it cool. Slit the skin of the tongue. Remove the root and skin the tongue.

Slice the boiled tongue and gently reheat in a small amount of hot water. Remove the slices from the water. Drain and arrange on a serving plate. Serve warm in sultana sauce or cold.

Sultana Sauce

1/2 cup raisins
1/2 cup hot water
1/4 cup vinegar
1/4 cup butter
2 tablespoons sugar
1/4 teaspoon salt
1/2 teaspoon each cinnamon, cloves, and allspice
2 tablespoons cornstarch
1/4 cup cold water

Place all the ingredients except the cornstarch and cold water in a saucepan. Bring to a slow boil, reduce the heat and let simmer for 3 minutes. Mix the cornstarch and water until smooth. Bring the raisin mixture to a boil, stir in the cornstarch, and continue to cook for 1 minute, stirring gently. If the resulting sauce is thicker than you like, add a little water. Yields approximately 1 cup.

Cold Tongue

1 tongue, prepared as above
1 cup water
1/2 cup vinegar
4 tablespoons sugar

Place all the ingredients in a saucepan, bring to a boil, and simmer for about 10 minutes. Remove the tongue from the liquid, drain, and chill. Slice in thin slices and serve on a chilled platter.

Serves 6 to 8.

ENGLESIDE, BEACH HAVEN, N. J.,
ROB'T B. ENGLE, Proprietor.

Is a new and handsome Ho'el, with the modern conveniences and appointments of a first-class house. Is beautifully located on an elevation, overlooking both Ocean and Bay, a fine view of which can be had from every bed-room in the house. The rooms are large and airy, and furnished with spring beds and hair mattresses. It is the nearest house to the beach in the place, and is one of the finest houses on the N. J. coast. Especial pains are always taken to have the table abundantly supplied with all the luxuries and delicacies of the place and season, and we challenge the world to produce *better* or *purer* drinking water than is furnished the guests of ENGLESIDE.

An advertisement for the Engleside Hotel, Beach Haven, around 1880. The Engleside prided itself on a table "abundantly supplied with the delicacies of the place and season." Because of Beach Haven's offshore location and pollen-free air, the Engleside was a favorite with hay-fever sufferers.

LAMB PIE

2 pounds lamb meat, boneless, cut for stewing
  or 3 cups leftover lamb, cut into 1-inch pieces
1/2 teaspoon salt
3 tablespoons flour
3 tablespoons shortening
12 small onions, boiled
4 medium potatoes, peeled, quartered, and cooked
1 1/2 cups small carrots, cooked
1/4 cup peas
2 cups lamb or beef broth or 2 cups leftover lamb
  gravy, heated
1/2 teaspoon salt (or to taste)
6 tablespoons flour
3 tablespoons vinegar
2 tablespoons sugar
2 tablespoons tomato catsup
3 drops Tabasco sauce
pastry to cover top of 9-to-10-inch casserole

Roll the raw lamb pieces in the salt and flour. Melt the shortening in a skillet and sauté the meat over low heat until brown and cooked through. (If using leftover lamb, omit this step.) Mix the meat, onions, potatoes, carrots, and peas, and place them in a deep 2 1/2-quart casserole.

Make a gravy by pouring 1 1/4 cups of the broth into the skillet in which the meat was sautéed. Let it boil gently a few minutes while scraping the pan. Add the salt. In a small bowl, mix the flour and remaining broth to a smooth paste. Gradually add the paste to the boiling liquid. Cook, stirring, until it thickens. If using heated, leftover gravy, omit this step. Add the vinegar, sugar, tomato catsup, and Tabasco sauce. Pour the gravy over the meat and vegetables in the casserole. Cover with pastry rolled to fit the top of the dish. Prick the pastry and bake at 425° for 20 minutes or until nicely browned.

Pastry

1/2 teaspoon salt
1 1/2 cups flour
1/2 cup shortening
3 tablespoons water

Add the salt to the flour. Mix well. Cut in the shortening. Add the water and mix lightly until all the flour is moistened. Press the dough into a ball. Roll out on a floured board to fit the casserole.

Serves 6.

~~~~~~

ROAST LEG OF LAMB WITH MINT SAUCE

In the United States lamb is a sheep that is less than one year old. The Victorians ate lamb well done. If you prefer lamb rarer, keep in mind that it may be infected with internal parasites.

1 5-to-8-pound leg of lamb
salt and black pepper (to taste)

Rinse the lamb. Season with salt and black pepper. Place the lamb on a rack in a shallow roasting pan. Roast at 325° for 40 minutes per pound or until a meat thermometer inserted into the thickest part of the leg registers 180°. After an hour, baste every half-hour.

You may need to add a little water to the roasting pan now and then to keep the roast from burning. Serve with mint sauce.

Mint Sauce

1 cup cider vinegar
3 tablespoons sugar
1/4 teaspoon salt
1/4 cup mint, chopped

In a small saucepan, put the vinegar, sugar, and salt. Cook over low heat, stirring frequently, until the mixture comes to a full boil. Remove it from the heat and let it cool for about 10 minutes. Add the mint and stir. Serve warm over lamb. Yields 1 cup.

Serves 7 to 8.

Driving on the beach at Cape May, 1895.

LAMB CHOPS MAINTENON

Named for the marquise de Maintenon (1635–1719), wife of King Louis XIV of France, this dish was served as an entrée at the Jersey Shore hotels. It was called "lamb chops farcie Maintenon" even though the chops are not actually stuffed (*farcie* in French).

8 rib lamb chops
1¼ teaspoons salt (or to taste)
¼ teaspoon black pepper
shortening
4 tablespoons butter
4 tablespoons flour
2 cups strong chicken broth
¼ cup onions, chopped fine and sautéed in butter
    until soft, transparent, and golden
⅓ cup mushrooms, chopped very fine and sautéed
    in butter for 5 minutes
8 tablespoons soft bread crumbs
⅓ cup melted butter
juice of ½ to 1 whole lemon (depending on taste)
4 egg yolks

Sprinkle the lamb chops lightly with a small part of the salt and black pepper. Melt the shortening in a frying pan. Sauté the lamb chops, on one side, over low heat for 10 minutes. Set aside.

In a saucepan, melt the butter. Gradually add the flour, stirring constantly, until the mixture is smooth and starts to bubble. Remove from the heat. Heat the chicken broth to boiling and gradually pour 1 cup into the butter and flour, stirring constantly to keep it smooth. Stir in $1/2$ teaspoon of the salt. Simmer for a few minutes over low heat, continuing to stir.

Measure out $1/2$ cup of the sauce and place it in a bowl. (Set the remaining sauce aside for now.) Add the onions and mushrooms. Mix well. Spread $1/8$ of the mixture on the cooked side of each lamb chop. Now sprinkle a tablespoon of bread crumbs on each lamb chop and top with $1^1/2$ teaspoons of the melted butter. Place the lamb chops in a roasting pan and bake at 375° for 30 minutes.

Reheat the remaining sauce over low heat. Reheat the remaining chicken broth. Gradually add the hot chicken broth to the sauce while beating well to keep it from lumping. Add the lemon juice and remaining salt and black pepper and bring to a boil, stirring constantly.

In a mixing bowl, beat the egg yolks. Gradually add the hot chicken broth sauce to the egg yolks, beating constantly. Return the sauce to the saucepan. Cook over low heat, stirring constantly, for about 2 minutes to thicken the sauce. If the sauce reaches a temperature of more than 175° on a candy thermometer, it will curdle.

Place the lamb chops under the broiler and broil for about 5 minutes or until the top is nicely browned.

To serve, you may wish to place a paper frill on the bone end of each chop. Frilled or not, place the lamb chops on a serving plate and serve with the sauce, which is a variation of sauce velouté.

Serves 4.

BREADED LAMB CUTLETS WITH TOMATO SAUCE

To give a formal, cosmopolitan flavor to its menu, the West End Hotel in Long Branch listed this dish as "cotelettes d'agneau pannes with sauce tomate." For less sophisticated diners it listed corned beef and baked pork and beans on the same menu.

4 to 8 lamb cutlets (depending on size)
salt and black pepper (to taste)
2 to 3 egg yolks, beaten
2 cups bread crumbs
shortening

Pound each cutlet to about ½ to ¾ inch thick. Sprinkle lightly with salt and black pepper. Dip each cutlet into the beaten egg yolks and then into the bread crumbs, coating well.

Melt the shortening in a heavy frying pan. Sauté the cutlets over low heat, turning often, until they are brown and cooked through. Serve warm with tomato sauce.

President Ulysses S. Grant's cottage, Long Branch, 1876.

Tomato Sauce

1 cup stewed tomatoes (canned or fresh)
1 onion slice
1 cup beef broth
2 teaspoons sugar
$1/2$ teaspoon salt (or to taste)
$1/4$ teaspoon black pepper
4 tablespoons butter
4 tablespoons flour
1 tablespoon vinegar

In a blender, blend the tomatoes and onion slice. (For a seedless sauce, sieve the tomato before blending it with the onion.) Pour into a saucepan and mix in the beef broth, sugar, salt, and black pepper. Heat to a slow boil.

In a saucepan, melt the butter over low heat, browning it lightly. Stir in the flour with a wooden spoon and cook, stirring constantly, until the mixture is smooth and starting to bubble. Pour in the tomato–beef broth mixture slowly, stirring vigorously. Boil slowly for 1 minute. Reduce the heat to a simmer. Add the vinegar and stir well. Continue to simmer for 10 minutes, stirring often. Pour the sauce over the lamb cutlets and serve at once. Yields 2 cups.

Serves 4.

President James A. Garfield's cottage, Long Branch, 1881. Gravely wounded by an assasin's bullet in Washington, D.C., President Garfield was transported to his cottage in the Elberon section of Long Branch but died there in September 1881 as a result of the wound.

BOILED LEG OF MUTTON WITH CAPER SAUCE OR SAUCE VÉNITIENNE

Mutton is the meat of a sheep that is more than one year old. The best mutton is called yearling and comes from a sheep that is between one and two years old.

1 9-to-12-pound leg of mutton
1 onion, sliced
½ lemon, sliced
1 bay leaf
1 teaspoon salt

Have the butcher trim the fat from the mutton. If the mutton is from a sheep more than two years old, have the butcher also remove the fell (the tissue on the surface of the leg). You may wish to have the butcher remove the shank end of the leg, and use only the butt end, depending on the size of the cooking pot available to you.

Rinse the meat and place it in a large kettle. Add the onion, lemon slices, and bay leaf. Cover the leg with boiling water. Bring quickly to a rolling boil and cook for 10 minutes. Skim off the fat. Reduce the heat and simmer for 30 minutes for each pound of mutton, or until tender. After 1 hour add the salt. When cooked, remove the mutton from the broth and place on a platter to await carving. Serve with a warm sauce.

Caper Sauce

4 tablespoons butter
4 tablespoons flour
2 cups mutton broth, strained and skimmed
1/2 teaspoon salt (or to taste)
1/8 teaspoon black pepper
1 tablespoon lemon juice
1/4 cup capers, drained

In a saucepan, melt the butter over low heat. Blend in the flour and cook, stirring constantly, until the mixture is smooth and starting to bubble. In a saucepan, bring the mutton broth to a boil. Slowly add it to the butter and flour, stirring vigorously as you pour. Bring to a boil. Add the salt and black pepper. Boil for 1 minute. Reduce the heat and simmer for 10 minutes. Remove from the heat and add the lemon juice and capers. Stir and serve at once. Yields 2 cups.

Sauce vénitienne

4 tablespoons butter
4 tablespoons flour
2 cups chicken broth
1/2 teaspoon salt
1/8 teaspoon white pepper
2 teaspoons tarragon vinegar
2 teaspoons chervil vinegar
1/4 cup butter
1/4 teaspoon each tarragon, thyme, and white pepper
2 tablespoons parsley, chopped

In a saucepan, melt the butter over low heat. Blend in the flour and cook, stirring constantly, until the mixture is smooth and starting to bubble. In a saucepan, heat the chicken broth to boiling. Slowly add it to the butter and flour, stirring vigorously as you pour. Bring to a boil. Add the salt and white pepper. Boil for 1 minute. Reduce the heat and simmer for 10 minutes, stirring frequently. Remove from the heat and add the two types of vinegar and the butter. Whip well. Add the tarragon, thyme, white pepper, and parsley. Whip well again. Serve at once. Yields 2 cups.

Serves 12 to 15.

VENISON STEAKS WITH CURRANT JELLY

Venison is the meat of the antelope, moose, and elk as well as the common deer. Charles Ranhofer recommended venison from deer between the ages of 18 months and $2\frac{1}{2}$ years: "Those with brown hair are better than those with red. Males over three years of age are unfit to eat in certain months of the year. The meats of the kid or doe are also excellent after they have attained the age of nine or ten months."

4 $\frac{1}{2}$-to-$\frac{3}{4}$-inch steaks, from the leg of a young deer
salt and black pepper
1 cup soft butter

Sprinkle each steak with salt and black pepper and dot with 2 tablespoons of butter. Broil from 3 to 4 minutes. Turn the steaks, sprinkle lightly with salt and black pepper, dot with 2 tablespoons of butter, and broil for 3 to 4 minutes. Serve with currant jelly or jelly sauce.

Currant Jelly Sauce

$\frac{1}{2}$ cup butter
$\frac{1}{2}$ cup currant jelly

While the steaks are broiling, melt the butter and jelly in a small saucepan. Stir well and serve with the venison. Yields 1 cup.

Serves 4.

An Atlantic City hotel lobby, 1874.

ROAST LOIN OF VEAL

Veal is beef from 4 to 14 weeks of age, the most desirable being from 6 to 8 weeks old. It is most commonly available in late winter and spring. Most of the veal available during the rest of the year is calf (beef from 14 weeks to 1 year old). Veal is always served well done.

1 3-to-4-pound loin of veal
1/2 teaspoon salt
1/4 teaspoon black pepper
6 strips fat bacon
1/4 teaspoon thyme

Rinse the veal and pat dry with a paper towel. Sprinkle the veal with the salt and black pepper. Place the meat on a rack in a shallow roasting pan. Arrange the bacon strips over the top of the veal. Sprinkle with the thyme. If you use a meat thermometer, insert it in the center of the thickest part of the veal. Place the veal in a 325° oven and roast, uncovered, for 35 minutes per pound or until a meat thermometer registers 170°. Serve warm with brown gravy or cold in thin slices.

Brown Gravy

4 tablespoons fat from the roasting pan
4 tablespoons flour
2 cups water
1/2 teaspoon salt
1/4 teaspoon black pepper
2 tablespoons vinegar
liquid gravy coloring (optional)

After the roast has been removed to a warm platter, take 4 tablespoons of fat from the roasting pan. Pour off the remaining fat. Place the roasting pan over low heat. Add the 4 tablespoons of fat and blend in the flour. Stir with a wooden spoon until the mixture is smooth and bubbling. Remove the pan from the heat and stir in the water, salt, and black pepper. Return to the heat and continue to cook, stirring constantly, until the gravy is smooth and thickened. Add the vinegar, more salt (if needed), and the liquid gravy coloring (if used). Let simmer for a few minutes, stirring frequently. Yields 2 cups.

Serves 8.

SHOULDER OF VEAL WITH HERB STUFFING

1 4-to-5-pound shoulder of veal
1 teaspoon salt
¼ cup butter, melted
¼ teaspoon black pepper
¾ cup beef broth
⅓ cup dry white wine

Have the butcher bone the shoulder of veal. Rinse the veal and pat dry. Rub ¼ teaspoon of the salt in the cavity. Spoon the stuffing into the cavity and sew up the opening. Place the shoulder on a rack in a shallow roasting pan. Pour the melted butter over the meat, turning to cover all sides. Pat the remaining salt and the black pepper on all sides of the buttered meat. Roast the shoulder at 300° for 3½ hours or until tender. Combine the beef broth and the white wine. Baste the veal with this liquid and the drippings from the roasting pan every 20 minutes. Serve with tomato sauce or brown gravy (recipe page 75).

Herb Stuffing

2 tablespoons butter
1 carrot, finely chopped
1 onion, finely chopped
¼ cup beef broth
2 cups bread crumbs
¼ cup cooked ham, finely chopped
1 egg, hard-cooked, finely chopped
1 tablespoon parsley, chopped
¼ teaspoon each, marjoram and thyme
¼ teaspoon salt
¼ teaspoon red pepper flakes

In a small frying pan, melt the butter and sauté the carrot and onion for 5 minutes over low heat. Add the beef broth and simmer for 5 minutes. In a mixing bowl, combine the bread crumbs, ham, egg, herbs, salt, and red pepper. Mix the broth into the bread crumb mixture. Spoon into the shoulder of veal. Yields approximately 2 cups.

Tomato Sauce

2¹/₂ cups canned tomatoes
1 cup beef broth
¹/₄ teaspoon thyme
¹/₄ teaspoon salt (or to taste)
1 tablespoon sugar
2 tablespoons vinegar
¹/₄ teaspoon black pepper
¹/₈ teaspoon cayenne pepper
¹/₄ cup butter
3 tablespoons flour

Press the tomatoes through a sieve to remove the seeds. Mix the pulp with the beef broth, thyme, salt, sugar, vinegar, black pepper, and cayenne pepper. Bring to a boil. Reduce the heat and simmer for 15 minutes.

In a saucepan, melt the butter over low heat. Blend in the flour, stirring constantly until it is smooth and bubbling. Remove from the heat and add the tomato purée slowly, stirring constantly until smooth. Return to low heat and simmer for 10 minutes, stirring frequently. Serve with stuffed shoulder of veal. Yields 2¹/₂ cups.

Serves 8 to 10.

On the veranda of the Ocean Hotel, Long Branch, 1872.

BLANQUETTE OF VEAL

2 pounds lean, boneless veal, cut into 2-inch cubes
6 cups water
1 carrot
2 onions
1/4 teaspoon thyme
1 3/4 teaspoons salt
1/2 cup butter
12 small onions
1 1/2 cups button mushrooms
3 tablespoons flour
2 cups veal broth
1/4 teaspoon white pepper
4 egg yolks
juice of 2 lemons
garnish: 2 tablespoons parsley, chopped

In a stewing pot, put the veal, 5 cups of the water, the carrot, onions, thyme, and 1 teaspoon salt. Bring to a boil. Cover tightly, reduce the heat, and simmer for 1 1/2 hours. Remove the veal, the carrot, and onions from the liquid. Keep the veal warm. Reserve the vegetables for another use.

In a saucepan, put 1/4 cup of the butter, the remaining 1 cup of water, 1/4 teaspoon of the salt, and the small onions. Bring to a boil. Cover tightly, reduce the heat, and simmer for 20 minutes. Stir. Add the mushrooms and more water, if necessary. (The onions should not brown.) Cover and simmer for 20 more minutes. Keep warm.

In a saucepan, melt the remaining butter. Blend in the flour and cook over low heat until the mixture is smooth and bubbling. Remove from the heat. Slowly add 2 cups of the broth from the veal, stirring until smooth. Return to the heat and bring to a boil. Add the remaining 1/2 teaspoon salt and the white pepper. Simmer for 5 minutes, stirring frequently.

In a bowl, beat the egg yolks well. Gradually add the hot liquid, beating constantly and vigorously. Return to the saucepan and add the lemon juice. Cook over low heat for 2 minutes, stirring constantly. Do not allow the sauce to exceed 175° on a candy thermometer to prevent curdling. Stir in onions and mushrooms with 1/4 cup of their cooking liquid.

Place the warm veal on a heated platter and pour the sauce over it. Garnish with the chopped parsley.

Serves 4.

FRICASSÉE OF VEAL

The Monmouth race course, 1886. A highlight of a Long Branch holiday was an excursion to the Monmouth horse races. The races were started in 1870 and drew a dazzling and flamboyant clientele.

2 cups water
2 onions, chopped
1 teaspoon salt
1/4 cup butter
1/4 cup flour
1 cup milk
1/2 cup light cream
1/2 cup onion broth
1/4 teaspoon black pepper
1/8 teaspoon cayenne pepper
3 cups cooked veal, cut into 1-inch pieces
1/2 cup cooked ham, chopped very fine

In a saucepan, bring the water to a boil and add the onions and 1/2 teaspoon of the salt. Reduce the heat, cover, and simmer for 1/2 hour. Strain out the onions and set aside. Reduce the broth to 1/2 cup.

In a saucepan, melt the butter and blend in the flour. Cook over low heat, stirring constantly, until the mixture is smooth and bubbling. (Do not let it brown.) Remove from the heat, add the milk, cream, and onion broth, and stir until smooth. Return to the heat and add the remaining 1/2 teaspoon of salt and the peppers. Stir in the veal, ham, and onions. Cook for 10 minutes over low heat, stirring often.

Serve over hot biscuits or toast with green peas on the side.

Serves 4 to 6.

FRICANDEAU OF VEAL WITH GREEN PEAS

A fricandeau is a meat dish, usually made of veal that has been larded and cooked by braising. Judging by the frequency with which recipes for fricandeau appear in the cookbooks of the time, it was a great favorite with Victorians. In the cookbooks of the era the directions for preparing a fricandeau of veal range from the long and complicated to a one line instruction in Fanny Farmer. There was disagreement over which cut of veal was the best to use.

1/4 pound fat salt pork
1 2 1/2-to-3-pound round or rump roast of veal
1/2 teaspoon salt (or to taste)
3 thin slices bacon
2 carrots, sliced
2 large onions, sliced
2 stalks celery, sliced
2 tablespoons parsley, chopped
1/4 teaspoon thyme
1/4 teaspoon white pepper
2 cups veal or chicken broth
1/2 cup dry white wine
1 1/2 cups green peas

Make lardons by removing any rind from the salt pork and cutting the pork into 1/4-inch-thick strips. Each strip should be about 2 inches long. If you freeze the lardons at this point, they will be easier to work with. When the lardons are firm, sprinkle the veal with 1/4 teaspoon of the salt. With a larding needle or small, sharp knife insert the lardons, 1 inch into the upper side of the veal. Leave 1 inch of each protruding from the surface of the veal. Lard with the grain of the meat and in parallel rows about 1 inch apart, starting from the center. (If the larding process seems too tedious, ask your butcher to do it for you. Or instead of larding the veal, you may place thin slices of salt pork over the meat. However, the results will not be the same.)

In a Dutch oven, first place the slices of bacon, then the vegetables and parsley. Sprinkle with the thyme, salt, and white pepper. Place the veal on the vegetables, larded side up, and add the broth. If necessary, add enough water to cover the vegetables. Cover tightly and simmer over low heat for 2 to 2 1/2 hours. Check occasionally to be sure there is enough liquid. Remove the veal and roast at 400° for 5 minutes to firm up the lardons. Remove at once and keep warm while you prepare the sauce.

To make the sauce, add the white wine to the Dutch oven. Stir. Strain out the vegetables and bacon. Discard the bacon. Remove as much fat from the liquid as possible. Put the vegetables through a sieve or purée them in a blender with a small amount of the liquid. Add the puréed vegetables to the liquid. If the sauce is too thick, add more white wine or broth. If it is too thin, thicken with a little flour and simmer over low heat for 5 minutes, stirring constantly. Correct the seasoning.

Serve the veal with either whole green peas, or puréed peas as the Victorians would have done. Place the fricandeau on a heated platter. Spoon some of the sauce over the veal and arrange the peas to one side. Serve the extra sauce in a sauceboat.

Serves 6.

A day at the Monmouth races, 1886. One observer noted that even the wealthy and elegantly dressed went to the races in an omnibus furnished by their hotel, instead of driving their private carriages. Decorum at the races was reportedly sedate, and betting was a serious business.

VEAL SWEETBREADS IN PUFF PASTRY

The West End Hotel in Long Branch offered this entrée to its guests in the 1870s under the name "vol-au-vent de ris de veau toulousaine." Traditionally the dish would have also included cockscombs.

6 puff pastry shells, frozen
2 pairs sweetbreads
2 chicken breasts
12 mushroom caps
1 cup dry white wine
1/2 cup water
1 celery rib, small onion, carrot, chopped
4 tablespoons butter
4 tablespoons flour
1 teaspoon salt
1/2 teaspoon white pepper
1 cup heavy cream
2 tablespoons dry sherry

Bake the puff pastry shells as directed on the package. Wipe clean the sweetbreads, chicken, and mushrooms. In a large saucepan combine the wine, water, celery, onion, and carrot and boil them for 5 minutes. Add the sweetbreads, chicken, and mushrooms to the liquid and poach gently 5 to 10 minutes or until cooked. The mushrooms may be removed before the meats. Cut the gristle from the sweetbreads and chicken, and slice uniformly. Strain the liquid and cook to reduce it to one cup.

Melt the butter in a saucepan, stir in the flour, salt, and white pepper and cook until it bubbles. Add the strained poaching liquid and heavy cream. Cook until thickened. Stir in the sherry.

Add the sweetbreads, chicken, and mushroom caps to the cream sauce, heat, and serve in the puff pastry shells.

Serves 6.

BOILED OR BAKED HAM WITH SAUCE

Pork, other than ham or bacon, seldom appeared on the menus of the shore hotels during the Victorian era. Fanny Farmer, in her cookbook of 1896, advised that pork was the most difficult meat to digest, therefore it should be "seldom served and then only during the winter months." However, the salting, curing, and smoking of hams made them "more wholesome." "Bacon," she said, "next to butter and cream, is the most easily assimilated of all fatty foods." She considered sugar-cured hams to be the best. All the hams at that time were purchased raw and required complete cooking in the kitchen, unlike today when cooked or partially cooked hams can be purchased.

Boiled Ham

1 12-to-14-pound country-style ham (uncooked)

Cover the ham with cold water and soak it for 24 to 36 hours, changing the water at least once during the soaking period.

Remove the ham from the water and scrub it thoroughly. Rinse well. Place the ham in a large kettle, cover it with cold water, and bring to a slow boil. Reduce the heat, cover, and let the ham simmer at the boiling point for 35 minutes per pound, or until the large bone in the heavy end of the ham becomes loose and is protruding. Remove the ham from the cooking water. Cut or pull off the rind and trim off any excess fat. Garnish the bone end with a paper ruffle, if desired. Serve the ham cold or hot with a sauce (recipes pages 84 and 85).

Baked Ham

1 12-to-14-pound country-style ham (uncooked)
whole cloves
1 cup sugar, brown or white
3 tablespoons prepared mustard
1 tablespoon honey

Cook the ham in the same manner as boiled ham. After the rind is removed, score the fat into diamonds. Stud each diamond with a clove. Mix the sugar, mustard, and honey, and spread the mixture over the ham. Bake in a 325° oven for 45 minutes. To serve, garnish the bone end with a paper ruffle, if desired. Serve the ham cold or hot with a sauce (recipes pages 84 and 85).

Cinnamon Sauce

2 tablespoons butter
2 tablespoons flour
$1/2$ cup boiling water
$1/2$ cup dry white wine
1 cup brown sugar
$1/4$ teaspoon salt
$1/2$ teaspoon cinnamon

In a saucepan, melt the butter. Add the flour and stir with a wooden spoon until the mixture is smooth and starting to bubble. Gradually add the water, then the wine, stirring constantly. Add the sugar, salt, and cinnamon. Stir well. Boil for 1 minute, stirring constantly, then lower the heat and simmer the sauce for 10 minutes, stirring often. Yields 1 cup.

Champagne Sauce

4 tablespoons butter
4 tablespoons flour
2 cups strong beef broth
$1/2$ teaspoon salt
$1/4$ teaspoon black pepper
$1/8$ teaspoon cloves
1 tablespoon sugar
$1/2$ cup champagne
1 tablespoon mushrooms, finely chopped and sautéed

In a saucepan, melt the butter. Gradually add the flour, stirring constantly to keep it from lumping. Allow the butter and flour to brown slightly. Gradually add the beef broth, stirring constantly until it is smooth and thickened. Add the salt and black pepper and let the sauce continue to cook until it has been reduced to $1^{1}/2$ cups. Remove the sauce from heat and add the cloves, sugar, champagne, and mushrooms. Stir well. Serve warm. Yields 2 cups.

Madeira Sauce

Prepare in the same manner as champagne sauce, but omit the cloves, sugar, and champagne. Add instead $1/4$ teaspoon of red pepper and $1/2$ cup of Madeira. Yields 2 cups.

Marsala Sauce

Prepare in the same manner as Madeira sauce but use ½ cup of Marsala instead of the Madeira. Yields 2 cups.

Serves 25.

GLAZED COLD HAM

1 12-to-14-pound ham
1²/₃ cups cold water
5 packets unflavored gelatin
2½ cups sugar
¹/₃ cup hot water
¼ teaspoon ground cloves
2 tablespoons prepared mustard

Cook a 12-to-14 pound ham. Score the fat, remove the rind, and cool. (Recipe page 83)

In a bowl, put 1 cup of the cold water, and sprinkle the gelatin over the water to soften. In a saucepan, put 1¼ cups of the sugar. Let it cook over low heat, stirring constantly, until it starts to brown and become like syrup. Remove it from the heat and gradually stir in the hot water, stirring constantly. Add the remaining sugar, cloves, and mustard. Stir well. Return the glaze to the heat and cook for 3 minutes longer, stirring vigorously. Remove the glaze from the heat. Add the gelatin and stir until it is completely dissolved. Add the remaining cold water. Stir, then let the mixture cool somewhat.

Spoon some of the gelatin over the top and sides of the ham, spreading evenly. Wait a few minutes and coat the ham a second time with the remaining gelatin. The glaze should be firm in about 30 minutes.

Serves 20 to 25.

ROAST SUCKLING PIG

Roast suckling pig was one of the few pork dishes included on the Jersey Shore hotel menus. The Dennis Hotel of Atlantic City offered this traditional holiday roast on Thanksgiving.

1 12-to-14-pound suckling pig
1/2 teaspoon salt
dressing (optional)
water
1 cup melted butter or sausage drippings
1 apple
2 cranberries
garnish: parsley or sage leaves

Rinse the pig well and sprinkle it with the salt. Stuff the pig with dressing, if desired, and sew up the opening. If you prefer the pig without dressing, stuff the abdominal cavity with crumpled aluminum foil so the pig will hold its shape.

Place the pig on a rack in a uncovered roasting pan. Extend the front feet forward and fold the hind feet under the pig. Place a wooden block in the mouth to keep it open. Cover the ears and tail with aluminum foil to keep them from burning. Prick the skin in a number of places.

Pour enough water into the roasting pan to cover the bottom. You will need to continue to add water to the roasting pan throughout the cooking period. Pour the melted butter or sausage drippings over the body of the pig. Roast at 325° for 35 minutes per pound of pig. Baste every half-hour with the water and drippings from the bottom of the roasting pan. Remove the aluminum foil from the ears and tail 30 minutes before the roasting time is up.

Place the pig on a platter. Remove the wooden block from the mouth and put in the apple. Place a cranberry in each eye socket. Surround the pig with parsley or sage leaves. Serve with gravy, if desired.

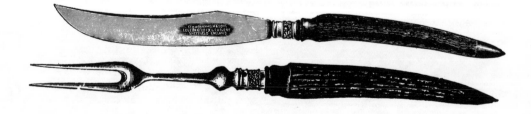

Dressing for Roast Suckling Pig

1 1/2 pounds white bread, crumbled
1/2 pound sausage, crumbled, thoroughly cooked,
   and drained of fat
1/2 cup onions, chopped fine and sautéed in
   5 tablespoons butter
2 cups apples, peeled and chopped
1/2 cup raisins
2 teaspoons dried sage
1 teaspoon salt
1/4 teaspoon black pepper
1 to 1 1/2 cups water

Mix all the ingredients together with just enough water to moisten. Stuff the cavity of the pig, sew up the opening, and bake. Any extra dressing may be baked separately.

Gravy for Roast Suckling Pig

1/2 cup pig fat
2 3/4 cups water
1/2 cup flour
1 teaspoon salt (or to taste)
1/4 teaspoon black pepper
1/8 teaspoon red pepper
1/4 cup vinegar

Pour off the fat from the roasting pan, reserving 1/2 cup. Pour the water into the roasting pan and bring to a boil slowly while scraping the browned particles.

In a saucepan, heat the fat over low heat and gradually add the flour, stirring constantly until the mixture is smooth and starting to bubble. Remove from the heat and gradually add the boiling water, stirring constantly. Return to the heat, bring to a boil, and cook for 1 minute, continuing to stir. Add the salt, peppers, and vinegar. Lower the heat and let the gravy simmer for 10 minutes, stirring often. You may add a little water if you like a thinner gravy. Adjust the seasonings. Yields approximately 3 cups.

Serves 20.

Bathing in the shade beneath the pier, Long Branch, 1879. Guide-
books of the period were quick to assure wary vacationers that
people were seldom injured while bathing in the surf, though one
author warned that the family doctor should be consulted about
the advisability of swimming in the open sea. Ocean bathing was
not recommended for the "weakly or timid" or for women and
children.

VEGETABLES

CORN O'BRIEN

This colorful dish was served at the Hotel Chelsea in Atlantic City. While this recipe calls for fresh corn, canned corn was widely available by 1870.

½ cup each sweet red and green peppers
¼ cup butter
2 cups fresh yellow corn (cut from 3 to 4 ears)
2 scallions, including greens, thinly cut
½ teaspoon salt (or to taste)
¼ teaspoon black pepper

In a skillet, sauté the peppers in the butter for 15 minutes over low heat. Stir often. Add the remaining ingredients and continue to sauté, stirring often, for another 5 minutes or until the corn is tender.

It was customary during the Victorian era to cook vegetables longer than we do today. If you wish to cook corn O'Brien in the Victorian style, add ¼ cup of water with the corn and cook for 20 minutes instead of 5, stirring often.

Serves 6.

STUFFED GREEN PEPPERS

Although the sweet green pepper was a native food of the Americas, first cultivated by pre-Incan Indians, it was widely grown in Europe before becoming popular in the United States during the Victorian era. Leland's Ocean House in Long Branch served them as an hors d'oeuvre, while the West End Hotel served them as an entrée under the name "poivres verts farci, à la Creole."

> 8 green peppers
> 1 cup chopped meat, cooked, or ³/₄ cup cooked sausage, crumbled, plus ¹/₄ cup chopped mushrooms
> 1 cup cooked rice
> ¹/₂ cup onions, finely chopped and sautéed
> 3 tomatoes, skinned and finely chopped (or 1 cup canned tomatoes)
> 1 teaspoon salt
> ¹/₈ teaspoon black pepper
> ¹/₄ teaspoon celery seeds
> 1 tablespoon vinegar
> 1 teaspoon sugar
> ¹/₄ cup water

Cut the tops from the green peppers and remove the seeds and membrane. Wash. Cook in boiling salted water for 5 minutes. Drain. (At this point a Victorian refinement was to allow the peppers to cool and then gently rub them with a soft cloth to remove the outer skin. However, Fanny Farmer, very sensibly, ignored this nicety.) Place peppers, open top up, in a well-greased baking dish.

Combine the remaining ingredients except the water. Mix well. Stuff the 8 peppers with the mixture. Pour water around peppers and bake at 350° for 30 minutes. (A century ago, the peppers would have been cooked for 45 to 50 minutes.)

Serves 8.

Ladies hiring bathing costumes at Long Branch, 1879. The usual women's bathing suit consisted of brown, blue, or gray flannel twill pantaloons and a coat or tunic, usually long-sleeved. Rubbers or sandals were recommended for protection from stones and crabs. A broad-brimmed hat was also *de rigeur*. Bathing costumes for men and women could be rented from beachside concessions like this one.

SAVORY POTATO CROQUETTES

Our word *croquette* comes from the French word *croquer*, meaning to crunch between one's teeth.

2 cups potatoes, mashed
1/2 teaspoon salt (or to taste)
1/4 teaspoon celery salt
1/8 teaspoon black pepper
2 tablespoons butter, melted
1/2 teaspoon onion, minced
1 egg yolk
2 eggs, beaten
fine bread crumbs
oil for frying

Combine all the ingredients except the beaten eggs and bread crumbs. Mix well and chill thoroughly. Shape the mixture into 8 balls, cones, or cylinders. Roll the croquettes in the bread crumbs. Chill again and dip in the beaten eggs. Roll in the bread crumbs again. Deep fry at 375° for 1 to 2 minutes or until golden brown. Drain on paper towels. Serve at once.

Serves 4 to 8.

POTATO CROQUETTES

These Victorian croquettes seem unusually sweet to the modern cook, who may only think of croquettes as a dish using leftovers. But they are delicious when well prepared. Victorian cooks garnished croquettes with a sprig of parsley and often served them with broiled chicken.

> 2 cups potatoes, mashed and salted to taste. (The
>   potatoes should be as dry as possible.)
> 2 tablespoons butter, melted
> 1/4 cup confectioners' sugar
> 1 teaspoon lemon peel, finely grated
> 1 egg yolk
> 2 eggs, beaten
> fine bread crumbs
> oil for frying

Mix the mashed potatoes with the butter, confectioners' sugar, lemon peel, and egg yolk. Chill thoroughly.

Shape the croquette mixture into 8 cones (prettier) or cylinders (easier). The cylinders should have flat ends. Roll the croquettes in the bread crumbs. Chill again for at least an hour.

Dip the croquettes in the beaten eggs and roll them in the bread crumbs again. It is important to crumb them well and evenly so that they do not become soggy with fat when frying. Deep fry at 375° for 1 to 2 minutes. If the fat is too hot the croquettes will not warm in the center. Drain on paper towels. Serve at once.

Serves 8.

POTATOES EN SURPRISE

Potatoes en surprise, a variation of croquettes, were served with the fish course at a gala wedding anniversary banquet in an Atlantic City hotel in 1901.

**2 cups savory potato croquette mixture, chilled
(recipe page 91)**
**½ cup filling: finely chopped, cooked chicken,
shrimp, egg yolk, or peas**
¼ cup cream
2 tablespoons butter
fine bread crumbs
2 eggs, beaten
oil for frying

Shape the croquette mixture into 8 balls. Push a hollow into each and fill with 1 tablespoon of either of the fillings. Add to each hollow 1 teaspoon of cream and a dot of butter. Close the balls. Roll them in bread crumbs and chill for 1 hour. Dip them in the beaten eggs and roll in the bread crumbs again.

Fry the balls in deep fat at 375° for 1 to 2 minutes or until golden brown. Drain on paper towels. Serve at once.

Serves 4 to 8.

Bathers receiving their valuables from the deposit safe at Long Branch, 1879.

The beach at Long
Branch, 1889.

POTATOES CHÂTEAU

4 cold boiled potatoes (cooked in salted water)
¹/₈ teaspoon black pepper
¹/₄ teaspoon onion powder
batter

Cut the potatoes in ¹/₄-inch slices. Sprinkle them with the black pepper and onion powder. Dip each slice in the batter. Deep fry at 375° until golden brown and drain on paper towels. Serve at once.

Batter

¹/₂ cup flour
¹/₂ teaspoon salt
¹/₄ teaspoon black pepper
¹/₃ cup milk
1 egg

Mix the flour, salt, and black pepper. Gradually add the milk, beating well. Add the egg and beat until the batter is smooth.

Serves 4.

POTATOES LONG BRANCH

A recipe for potatoes Long Branch appears in *The Epicurean* by Charles Ranhofer, the famous chef of Delmonico's in New York City. Potatoes Long Branch were also called curled potatoes.

2 large, long potatoes, peeled
oil for frying
salt (to taste)

Pare each potato into one long curl. If you are successful in keeping the curl intact, it may be a yard or two long. Soak the curls in cold water for 2 hours. Drain and dry them well. Deep fry them at 370° until they are crisp and golden brown. Carefully remove them from the fat and drain them on paper towels. Sprinkle with salt and serve at once.

Serves 2.

SARATOGA CHIPS

Though these chips were created in the rival resort of Saratoga Springs, New York, by chef George Crum, they were popular at the Jersey Shore too. Perhaps potatoes Long Branch were created to outdo them.

3 medium baking potatoes, peeled
oil for frying
salt

Slice the potatoes very thin with a vegetable peeler into iced water. Allow the potatoes to soak for one hour in this very cold water. Drain and pat the potatoes very dry.

In a deep saucepan, heat the oil slowly to 380°. Fry a few chips at a time until golden. Stir carefully to prevent them from sticking together. Drain on paper towels and sprinkle with salt, if desired.

Yields approximately 5 cups.

POTATOES HOLLANDAISE

4 potatoes
chicken stock, salted to taste
1/2 cup butter, softened
2 tablespoons lemon juice
1/4 teaspoon salt
1/8 teaspoon cayenne pepper
garnish: 1 tablespoon parsley, chopped

Peel the potatoes and cut them into 1/4-inch slices, or cut them into inch-thick balls with a melon cutter. Put the potatoes in a saucepan, cover them with the chicken stock, and bring to a boil. Cover and boil gently until the potatoes are soft, about 25 to 30 minutes. Do not overcook. Drain. (The remaining stock can be used in soup.)

Cream together the butter, lemon juice, salt, and cayenne pepper and add to the drained potatoes. Cook gently for 3 minutes. Stir gently. Pour into a serving dish. Garnish with the chopped parsley.

Serves 4.

HASHED POTATOES IN CREAM

Hashed potatoes in cream is a splendid dish in which to use last night's leftover potatoes. The Hotel Albion in Atlantic City served them for breakfast.

4 potatoes, peeled, cooked in salted water
3 tablespoons butter
1 tablespoon flour
1/4 teaspoon salt (or to taste)
1 cup light cream
1/8 teaspoon each black and cayenne pepper

Dice the potatoes and arrange them in a generously buttered baking dish. Make a sauce by melting 1 tablespoon of the butter in a saucepan. Blend in the flour and cook over low heat until smooth. Stir in the cream and bring to a slow boil, stirring constantly. Add the salt and the black and cayenne pepper.

Pour the sauce over the potatoes and dot with the remaining butter. Bake at 350° for 30 minutes.

Serves 4.

~~~~~~

NEW POTATOES IN CREAM

12 small new potatoes, or boiled potatoes, diced
1 teaspoon salt
2 tablespoons butter
2 tablespoons flour
1/2 teaspoon salt
1/4 teaspoon white pepper
1 cup light cream
garnish: 1/4 cup parsley, chopped, or grated cheese

Scrub the new potatoes and peel one strip around the
middle. Place the potatoes in a small saucepan and barely
cover with water. Add the salt and cover. Boil 15 to 25 minutes or until the potatoes are just tender. Drain and keep
them warm.

Melt the butter in a saucepan, stir in the flour, salt, and
white pepper and cook until it thickens. Whisk in the light
cream and cook until it is smooth and thick. Add the cooked
potatoes and warm gently.

To serve, garnish with the chopped parsley or grated
cheese.

On the beach, 1897.

Serves 6.

A bathing scene, 1886.

POTATO SALAD

6 medium potatoes, new or red
5 tablespoons salad oil
2 tablespoons lemon juice
1 teaspoon salt
$1/2$ teaspoon black pepper
1 tablespoon scallions, chopped
$1/4$ cup watercress or dandelion greens, chopped
$1/2$ cup mayonnaise
$1/2$ cup sour cream

Boil the potatoes in their jackets. When tender but not mushy, drain and cool them slightly. When the potatoes are cool enough to handle, remove the skin and slice carefully.

Combine the oil, lemon juice, salt, black pepper, and chopped vegetables. Toss this mixture carefully with the warm sliced potatoes. Refrigerate this salad. Just before serving, stir in the mayonnaise and sour cream.

Serves 6 to 8.

MASHED POTATO SALAD

Potato salad originated in the Teutonic countries after the white potato became an acceptable food in the late eighteenth century. By the Victorian era it had become a standard supper dish at the Jersey Shore hotels. Mashed potato salad is seldom served today. But it was very popular at the turn of the century.

6 medium potatoes, peeled
3/4 to 1 cup mayonnaise (depending on the dryness
  of the potatoes)
1/4 cup milk
2 tablespoons mustard
2 tablespoons vinegar
1 tablespoon sugar
1/2 teaspoon salt
1/4 teaspoon black pepper
4 hard-cooked eggs, chopped fine
1 Bermuda onion, chopped fine
2 stalks celery, chopped fine
garnish: parsley and paprika

Boil the potatoes in salted water until tender. Drain. Place the potatoes in a mixing bowl and mash. Add the mayonnaise, milk, mustard, vinegar, sugar, salt, and black pepper. Beat well. Whip in the eggs, onion, and celery.

Mound the salad on a plate and smooth it with a knife. To garnish, place the parsley generously around the base of the potato salad and sprinkle the mound generously with paprika. Chill.

Serves 6.

The dining room of the
West End Hotel, Long
Branch, 1875.

CREAMED ONIONS

18 to 24 small white onions
1 teaspoon salt
2 tablespoons butter
2 tablespoons flour
1/4 teaspoon salt
1/4 teaspoon white pepper
3/4 cup light cream
mace or nutmeg (optional)

Peel the onions carefully but do not remove all of the root end. This will prevent the onions from popping apart as they boil. In a small saucepan, barely cover the onions with water, add the salt, cover, and cook until just tender. Remove the onions from the pan and keep them warm. Boil the liquid until it is reduced to 1/4 cup.

In a saucepan, melt the butter. Stir in the flour, salt, and white pepper and cook until it thickens. Whisk in the reserved onion liquid and light cream and cook until it is thickened. Correct the seasonings if necessary. Add the cooked onions and heat gently. Top the serving dish with a sprinkle of mace or nutmeg.

Serves 6.

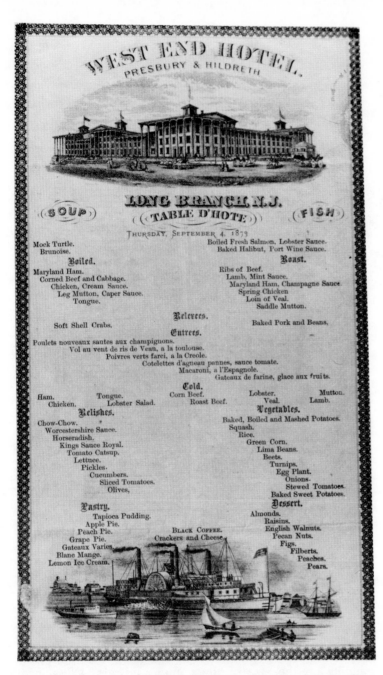

WEST END HOTEL
PRESBURY & HILDRETH

LONG BRANCH, N.J.
(((TABLE D'HOTE)))

((SOUP))   ((FISH))

THURSDAY, SEPTEMBER 4, 1873

Mock Turtle.
Brunoise.

Boiled Fresh Salmon, Lobster Sauce.
Baked Halibut, Port Wine Sauce.

Boiled.

Maryland Ham.
Corned Beef and Cabbage.
Chicken, Cream Sauce.
Leg Mutton, Caper Sauce.
Tongue.

Roast.

Ribs of Beef.
Lamb, Mint Sauce.
Maryland Ham, Champagne Sauce.
Spring Chicken
Loin of Veal.
Saddle Mutton.

Releves.

Soft Shell Crabs.

Baked Pork and Beans,

Entrees.

Poulets nouveaux sautes aux champignons.
Vol au vent de ris de Veau, a la toulouse.
Poivres verts farci, a la Creole.
Cotelettes d'agneau pannes, sauce tomate.
Macaroni, a l'Espagnole.
Gateaux de farine, glace aux fruits.

Cold.

Ham.   Tongue.   Corn Beef.   Lobster.   Mutton.
Chicken.   Lobster Salad.   Roast Beef.   Veal.   Lamb.

Relishes.

Chow-Chow.
Worcestershire Sauce.
Horseradish.
Kings Sauce Royal.
Tomato Catsup.
Lettuce.
Pickles.
Cucumbers.
Sliced Tomatoes.
Olives,

Vegetables.

Baked, Boiled and Mashed Potatoes.
Squash.
Rice.
Green Corn.
Lima Beans.
Beets.
Turnips.
Egg Plant.
Onions.
Stewed Tomatoes.
Baked Sweet Potatoes.

Pastry.

Tapioca Pudding.
Apple Pie.
Peach Pie.
Grape Pie.
Gateaux Varies.
Blanc Mange.
Lemon Ice Cream.

BLACK COFFEE.
Crackers and Cheese.

Dessert.

Almonds.
Raisins.
English Walnuts.
Pecan Nuts.
Figs.
Filberts.
Peaches,
Pears.

The dinner menu for Thursday, September 4, 1873, from the West End Hotel. Located in Long Branch, the West End Hotel was one of the best known Jersey Shore hotels in the 1870s. It catered to the wealthy and "those who [liked] to be in the whirl of a 'fashionable' watering place." Foreign ministers, senators, and congressmen reportedly stayed at the West End Hotel. (Courtesy, Special Collections, Alexander Library, Rutgers University)

Promenading on the beach at Cape May, 1875.

BROWNED SWEET POTATOES

The sweet potato is another of the native foods of the Americas, where it had been cultivated by the Indians long before the coming of Columbus. The Spanish brought it to Europe, where it was received immediately with great favor. From Europe it was introduced to the South Sea Islands and to Asia. The Victorian seaside hotels served them either boiled, baked, browned, or candied.

6 sweet potatoes
¹/₂ teaspoon salt
¹/₂ cup sugar
3 tablespoons butter
¹/₄ cup medium sherry (or water)

Scrub the sweet potatoes well. Place them in a saucepan and cover with boiling water. Cover and boil until the potatoes are tender. (This will take from 25 to 40 minutes depending on the size of the potatoes.) Drain. When cool enough to handle, peel and cut the potatoes into inch-thick slices.

Arrange the slices in a well-greased, shallow baking dish. Sprinkle them with the salt and sugar. Dot with butter. Pour the sherry (or water) over all. Bake at 375° for 20 to 25 minutes or until nicely browned on top.

Serves 6.

CANDIED SWEET POTATOES

Although seemingly the quintessential Victorian dish, the candied sweet potato has its roots in colonial America, where boiled-down maple syrup was used for candying. Remember that sweet potatoes are always best when cooked unpeeled.

6 medium sweet potatoes
3/4 cup brown sugar
1/3 cup water
3 tablespoons butter
1/2 teaspoon cinnamon
1/4 teaspoon ginger
mace and nutmeg (optional)

Wash the potatoes and boil them until they are tender. Drain, peel, and slice them crosswise into 1-inch slices. Overlap the slices in a shallow casserole or pie plate. Combine the sugar and water and bring to a boil. Pour the syrup over the potatoes, dot with the butter, and sprinkle with the spices. Bake at 400° for 20 minutes. Baste the potatoes occasionally with the syrup.

Serves 6.

A bathing scene, 1881. "By beginners, a bath should not be taken oftener than twice or thrice a week . . . If, after leaving the water, the lips are blue and lassitude ensues the bath should either have been omitted altogether or made briefer."

SCALLOPED TOMATOES

Scalloped tomatoes were one of the most popular ways to serve this New Jersey vegetable at the Jersey Shore hotels.

1 cup bread crumbs
1/4 cup butter, melted
2 cups canned tomatoes, drained and sliced (or 6
    fresh ripe tomatoes, skinned and sliced)
1/2 teaspoon onion powder
1 tablespoon sugar
1 teaspoon salt (or to taste), if using fresh tomatoes
1/8 teaspoon black pepper

Generously butter a shallow, 1- or 1 1/2-quart baking dish. Mix the bread crumbs and melted butter. Spread half of the bread crumb mixture on the bottom of the buttered baking dish. Spread the tomatoes over the layer of bread crumbs. Sprinkle the tomatoes with the onion powder, sugar, salt, and black pepper. Spread the rest of the bread crumb mixture over the layer of tomatoes. Bake at 350° for 25 to 30 minutes.

Serves 6.

STEWED TOMATOES

Tomato growing was well established in New Jersey by Victorian times, and no menu seemed complete without a tomato dish. In the 1870s, the Camden firm of Anderson and Campbell successfully canned the beefsteak tomato, assuring its availability throughout the year. They packed their tomatoes one to a can and advertised with a picture of two men carrying one enormous tomato.

2 1/2 cups canned tomatoes, including juice (or 6
    fresh ripe tomatoes, skinned and quartered)
1 tablespoon onion, finely chopped
3 tablespoons butter
2 tablespoons sugar
1/8 teaspoon black pepper
1 teaspoon salt (or to taste) if using fresh tomatoes
2 tablespoons flour

Drain ¼ cup of tomato juice from the canned tomatoes and set it aside. If you are using fresh tomatoes, measure out 3 tablespoons of water and set it aside. In a saucepan, put the tomatoes, onions, butter, sugar, black pepper, and salt (if any). Bring to a boil. Cover and reduce the heat. Simmer for 20 minutes, stirring often. Mix the flour and reserved tomato juice or water. Stir it into the hot tomatoes. Boil for 3 minutes or so, stirring constantly to avoid lumping and burning.

Serves 6.

STUFFED TOMATOES

It is said that stuffed tomatoes were one of President Millard Fillmore's favorite foods.

6 medium tomatoes
2 tablespoons butter
3 tablespoons onion, chopped
1 cup fresh bread crumbs
1 teaspoon salt
½ teaspoon black pepper
dash of cayenne pepper
1 teaspoon lemon juice
2 tablespoons butter

Cut a slice from the stem end of each tomato. With a spoon, gently remove the seeds and watery pulp. Melt the butter in a small saucepan and lightly sauté the onion. Add the bread crumbs and stir until brown and crisp. Add the salt, black and cayenne pepper, and lemon juice. Fill the tomatoes with the crumb mixture and dot the tops with butter.

Place the tomatoes in a baking pan and bake at 350° for 15 to 20 minutes.

Serves 6.

The first swim, 1879.

BREADS

BISCUITS

Biscuits, in one form or another, have always been a part of American cuisine. However, it was not until baking powder became available that the biscuit we know today became possible.

It was in Boston in 1855 that baking powder was first marketed. It would take another 20 to 30 years before it became universally available and accepted. As late as the 1880s, cookbooks still contained recipes to make baking powder at home.

Early baking powder was of the tartrate variety, so when adapting recipes of the period the amount of baking powder called for should be halved if today's double-acting baking powder is used (as it is in all the recipes in this book).

2 cups flour
3 teaspoons baking powder
1/2 teaspoon salt
3 tablespoons butter
1 cup milk

Mix the flour, baking powder, and salt thoroughly. Cut in the butter with a knife. Add the milk. Mix lightly and quickly with a large spoon.

Turn the dough out onto a well-floured bread board. Spread the top of the dough with flour and roll out to the thickness of 1/2 inch. Cut with a large biscuit cutter.

Place on a well-greased baking sheet. Bake at 450° for 15 minutes or until done.

Yields 12 biscuits.

SHORT BISCUITS

2 cups flour
2 teaspoons baking powder
1/2 teaspoon salt
1/2 cup shortening
3/4 cup plus 2 tablespoons milk

Sift the flour, baking powder, and salt into a mixing bowl. Add the shortening and cut it in with a knife. Add the milk. Mix lightly and quickly with a large spoon. Handle as little as possible.

Turn the dough out onto a well-floured board. Roll out the dough to the thickness of 1/3 to 1/2 inch. Cut with a small biscuit cutter (1 1/2 inches in diameter). Place on a greased baking sheet. Bake at 475° for 10 minutes or until crisp and lightly browned.

Yields 36 biscuits.

BREAD GRIDDLECAKES

These delicious pancakes were an excellent way for chefs to use leftover breads.

1/2 cup currants
1 cup water, boiling
1/2 cup flour
3 teaspoons baking powder
1/2 teaspoon salt
1 1/2 cups stale-bread crumbs
2 eggs, beaten
1 1/2 cups milk
2 tablespoons butter, melted

Soak the currants in the boiling water. Sift together the flour, baking powder, and salt, and stir in the bread crumbs. Combine the eggs and milk, and beat into the flour mixture. Stir in the butter and currants, which have been well drained. Bake on a lightly greased hot griddle. Serve with syrup, honey, or jam.

Yields 20 griddlecakes.

CORN BREAD

An American favorite since the earliest days of settlement, corn bread was served at the first Thanksgiving feast in Plymouth. The early colonial corn breads were often coarse and flat, cooked in the ashes or on the blade of a hoe. By the Victorian era, with the development of baking powder and soda and the addition of sugar, corn bread had become almost cake-like in comparison with the early cornbreads.

2 cups white cornmeal
1 teaspoon baking powder
1/2 teaspoon baking soda
2 tablespoons sugar
1 teaspoon salt
3 tablespoons butter, melted
1 1/4 cups buttermilk
2 eggs, beaten

Mix the cornmeal, baking powder, baking soda, sugar, and salt thoroughly. Add the butter and buttermilk. Beat well. Add the eggs and beat well until the batter is smooth. Pour into a well-greased 9-inch cake pan or iron skillet. Bake at 425° for about 25 minutes or until done. Turn out onto a serving plate and cut into 8 pieces.

Serves 8.

The New Columbia
House, Cape May, 1874.

POPOVERS

Believed by some to be an American creation, the popover is leavened by steam and requires a hot oven so steam will form rapidly. Recipes for popovers appeared in cookbooks from the 1870s.

2 eggs
1 cup milk
1 cup flour
¼ teaspoon salt

Beat the eggs slightly, then beat in the milk. Add the flour and salt. Whisk vigorously until the batter is smooth (about 2 minutes). Do not overbeat. (If you use an electric beater, beat no more than 50 seconds.) The batter should be the thickness of heavy cream. Too thick a batter will keep the popovers from rising.

Divide the batter into a well-greased popover pan or a 12-cup muffin pan. Cast-iron popover pans give the best results, but heavy aluminum pans or 8 well-greased custard cups may also be used. Bake in a pre-heated 425° oven for about 40 minutes. Serve at once.

Yields 8 to 12 popovers.

ALMOND ZWIEBACK

A sweetened "twice baked" toast, zwieback became popular in the late nineteenth century and was recommended as a first solid food for infants. It appeared on the hotel breakfast menus of the period.

1/2 cup butter

3/4 cup sugar

3 eggs

1/2 teaspoon vanilla

3 cups flour, sifted

1 tablespoon baking powder

1/2 teaspoon salt

1 cup almonds, finely chopped

2 tablespoons lemon rind, grated

1 teaspoon mace

In a large bowl, cream together the butter and sugar until the mixture is light and fluffy. Beat in the eggs, one at a time, and stir in the vanilla. Sift together the flour, baking powder, and salt and stir gradually into the butter mixture. Add the almonds, lemon rind, and mace. Form the dough into a ball, wrap in plastic, and chill for 1 hour.

Divide the dough into thirds and shape each piece into 1 1/2-inch-thick logs. Arrange the logs well apart on a greased baking sheet and flatten them to slightly less than 1 inch thick. Bake at 350° for 15 to 20 minutes. Remove from the oven and cool the loaves on the baking sheet.

Cut the cool loaves crosswise into 3/4-inch slices. Arrange the slices, cut side down, on a greased baking sheet. Bake at 350° for 20 to 24 minutes until golden and dry.

Yields 36 zwieback.

An Atlantic City hotel veranda, 1874. Open to the sea, the hotels afforded guests cool breezes to counteract the summer heat. In a storm, however, "the frame hotels quiver[ed] and rattl[ed] and shed clapboards in a most surprising way."

RAISED BISCUITS

Yeast is one of the oldest leavening agents we have, but it was always difficult to control and the results were always chancy. Around 1850 commercially compressed yeast was developed. However, like baking powder, it would be another 20 to 30 years before it became widely available and accepted. Cookbooks written during this period strongly urge the readers to forget homemade yeast and take advantage of this wonderful new product.

The recipe below calls for dry yeast because it is now more widely available than compressed. If possible, use preservative-free dry yeast. If you wish to use fresh yeast, you may substitute 1/2 ounce of fresh yeast for the package of dry yeast. Remember that yeast is a living organism and will be killed by excessive heat.

1 packet dry yeast
1/4 cup water, lukewarm
3/4 cup milk
1/4 cup butter
2 tablespoons sugar
1 teaspoon salt
3 cups flour
1/3 cup butter, melted

Add the yeast to the lukewarm water and let it stand for fifteen minutes. Heat the milk to the boiling point. Remove from the heat and add the butter, sugar, and salt. Let cool until lukewarm (90°) and then add the yeast. Stir and add the flour. Mix well and knead until the dough is smooth. Put the dough in a large greased bowl. Cover and let rise in a warm place until double in size.

Turn the dough onto a floured bread board. Roll out to the thickness of 1/2 inch. Cut with a small biscuit cutter. Place the biscuits 1 inch apart on a greased baking sheet. Brush with melted butter. Let rise for 45 minutes in a warm place. Bake at 400° for 15 to 20 minutes or until done.

Yields 24 biscuits.

BREAKFAST ROLLS

1 packet dry yeast

$1/4$ cup water, lukewarm

$3/4$ cup milk

$1/4$ cup butter

$1^1/2$ tablespoons sugar

$1/2$ teaspoon salt

$1/2$ teaspoon mace

3 cups flour, sifted

1 egg, beaten

$1/3$ cup butter, melted

Soften the yeast in the water. Heat the milk to the scalding point. Melt the butter in the warm milk, add the sugar, salt, and mace to the milk, and cool to lukewarm (105° to 110°). Place 1 cup of the flour in a bowl and stir in the yeast mixture. Add the egg and the remaining flour alternately, mixing well.

Place the dough in a greased bowl, cover, and let it rise in a warm place until double in bulk, about $1/2$ hour. Punch the dough down and let it rise again, about $1/2$ hour. Break off small pieces of dough and roll them into balls. Place them in greased muffin pans and brush with melted butter. Cover and let rise in a warm place until double in bulk, about 20 minutes. Bake at 425° for 15 minutes.

Leftover rolls may be transformed into zwieback by slicing and toasting them in a slow oven (250° to 275°) for $3/4$ to 1 hour or until evenly browned and dry, turning occasionally.

Yields 24 rolls.

ENTIRE WHEAT BREAD

Entire wheat bread appeared often on the breakfast menus of the Jersey Shore hotels. It was believed to be especially good for "persons who lead sedentary lives." Entire wheat bread rises little or not at all during baking, but it makes a handsome loaf that tastes and smells delicious. In this recipe the flour is warmed. *The Buckeye Cookbook* (1883) advises, warm the flour by "placing it in a pan in a *warm* oven for a few minutes." It was a common belief that it was unhealthy for a yeast bread to sit long before baking. It was thought the "sweet flavor" and "nutritious qualities" would suffer from a second "fermentation." Therefore, this recipe has only one rising.

> 3 cups whole wheat flour, slightly warm to the
>   touch (under 90°)
> 1 teaspoon salt
> 1⅓ cups water, heated to 90°
> 1 packet dry yeast
> 1 tablespoon sugar
> ⅓ cup whole milk, heated to 90°

In a mixing bowl, mix the flour and salt well. In a small bowl, pour ⅓ cup of the water. Sprinkle the yeast on top and let the yeast sit for 2 to 3 minutes. Add the sugar and let it stand for another 10 to 15 minutes. Stir. Add the yeast, the milk, and the remaining water to the flour. Mix well. It is not necessary to knead the dough. Put the dough into a well-greased and lightly floured 5x9x3-inch loaf pan or one that holds 8 cups. Let the bread rise in a warm place for 50 minutes.

Bake at 375° for 50 to 55 minutes. Turn the loaf out onto a rack to cool. If it is cut with a very sharp bread knife, it can be served at once.

Yields 1 loaf.

GRAHAM BREAD

Sylvester Graham (1794–1851) was a Presbyterian minister who believed that Americans were "digging their graves with their teeth." So he formulated a regimen of eating designed to improve the health and morals of the nation. Citing Genesis 1:29 ("And God said, Behold, I have given you every herb bearing seed, which is upon the face of all the earth, and every tree, in the which is the fruit of a tree yielding seed; to you it shall be for meat,") all meats, seafood, fats, sauces, gravies, and condiments were prohibited. Also proscribed were all liquids during the meal, including soups and water. Food was to be served cold or tepid. All alcoholic beverages were absolutely forbidden at all times.

Central to the approved Graham diet was bread or crackers baked with a coarse, unsifted flour made from the whole grain of wheat. The bread was not to be eaten until it was at least one day old.

Graham attracted many followers and even after his death in 1851, "Grahamism" continued to influence the American diet for at least another 50 years. And the crackers and flour that bear his name are still popular today.

2 cups Graham flour
1 teaspoon baking powder
1 teaspoon baking soda
2 tablespoons sugar
1 teaspoon salt
3 tablespoons butter, melted
1/4 cup molasses
1 egg, beaten
1 3/4 cups buttermilk

Mix together well the Graham flour, baking powder, baking soda, sugar, and salt. Combine the butter, molasses, egg, and buttermilk. Stir the liquid into the dry ingredients, mixing quickly and well. Pour into a well-greased 9x5x3-inch loaf pan. Bake at 350° for 1 hour or until done. Cool before slicing.

Yields 1 loaf.

The dinner hour at a Cape May hotel, 1871. Family dinner was
not necessarily the elegant affair touted in hotel promotions.

DESSERTS

BLANCMANGE

Blancmange, French for "white food," developed in the Middle Ages but not as a dessert. By the seventeenth century, however, it had become a gelatin dessert made with sweetened white wine and ground almonds. Some Victorian cookbooks continued to favor the older gelatin type, but most preferred to use the more fashionable cornstarch method of making blancmange.

1/4 cup sugar
4 tablespoons cornstarch
1/8 teaspoon salt
2 cups milk
1/2 teaspoon almond flavoring (optional)
1 cup strawberries or raspberries, crushed and
    sweetened to taste (or 4 tablespoons strawberry
    or raspberry preserves)

In the top half of a double boiler, combine the sugar, cornstarch, and salt. Mix with 1/2 cup of the milk to make a smooth paste. In a saucepan, bring the remaining milk to a slow boil, stirring constantly. Gradually stir the boiling milk into the cornstarch mixture. Mix well. Cook the blancmange over boiling water, stirring constantly, until smooth and thickened. Cover the top of the double boiler and cook for 10 minutes longer, stirring every 2 minutes. Remove from the heat and add the almond flavoring, if desired.

Rinse 4 1/2-cup molds or custard cups with cold water. Pour in the blancmange and chill. Unmold onto serving plates and serve with the crushed berries or berry preserves.

Serves 4.

CHARLOTTE RUSSE

1 package lady fingers or sponge cake
1 package unflavored gelatin (1 tablespoon)
¼ cup water
½ cup milk, scalded
½ teaspoon almond extract
1 cup heavy cream, whipped
garnish: maraschino cherries

Line a 1-quart charlotte mold or bowl with lady fingers or slices of sponge cake. Soak the gelatin in the water. When softened dissolve it in the hot milk. Fold in the almond extract and cool. Do not allow it to set. Fold in the whipped cream and pour into the prepared mold. Chill thoroughly until set. Unmold and garnish with maraschino cherries.

Serves 6.

The Stockton House, Cape May, 1874. It was said that the dining hall of the Stockton accomodated 800 guests. In 1875, *Lippincott's Magazine* commented that these guests were "fed with choice provisions from one of the richest markets in the world, served in their prime. They have been lodged in pretty rooms fitted with walnut furniture. The mattresses have been springy and devoid of lumps. The dining-room is a rich flower garden, where crystal and silver perennially bloom on beds of soft rich tablecloth; warm relays of delicate food, appreciated by pursy, unctuous gourmands, succeed each other day and evening. The balls are gay and crowded, the society is good."

FRASCATI GLACÉ

Frascati was a very popular café that opened in Paris after the French Revolution. It catered to the *nouveaux riches* who came to gossip and dance, eat ice cream, and sip liqueurs.

    1 quart vanilla ice cream
    5 tablespoons and 1/3 cup liqueur (Grand Marnier
       works very well.)
    8 macaroons
    8 candied cherries

Soften the ice cream and divide it into 8 sherbet glasses. Pack the ice cream down and smooth the top. Put the glasses in the freezer until firm. (It should not be frozen hard.) From the center of each glass remove enough ice cream to leave a hollow about 1½ inches wide and ¾ inch deep. Return the ice cream to the freezer.

Allow the scooped-out ice cream to soften and mix it with the 5 tablespoons of liqueur. Fill up the hollows with the mixture and return the glasses to the freezer. (You will have some of the ice cream–liqueur mixture left over.)

Soak each of the macaroons with some of the remaining liqueur. The macaroons should be semi-soaked but hold their shapes. Place a soaked macaroon over each filled hole of ice cream. Top each macaroon with a candied cherry. Return to the freezer until ready to serve.

Let the frascati glacé sit for a few minutes at room temperature before serving. The ice cream should be firm but not frozen hard.

Serves 8.

MARASCHINO CREAM IMPERIAL

Maraschino is a liqueur made from the marasca cherry. The original maraschino cherries were made by soaking cherries in maraschino liqueur.

1 quart almond ice cream
1½ cups vanilla ice cream (approximately)
1 cup cherry ice cream
1 cup rice pudding (recipe page 135)
½ cup macaroon crumbs
2 tablespoons maraschino liqueur or 2 tablespoons
   maraschino cherry liquid
1 cup heavy whipping cream
4 tablespoons confectioners' sugar (or to taste)
6 maraschino cherries, finely chopped

Let the almond ice cream soften so that it can be spread. Chill a 2-quart mold or an 8-cup metal mixing bowl. Line the mold or bowl with the softened almond ice cream. Place in the freezer until firm. Soften the vanilla ice cream. Remove the mold from the freezer and put ¾ cup of the softened vanilla ice cream into the hollow shell of almond ice cream, making a first layer. Return the mold to the freezer until the ice cream is frozen. Soften the cherry ice cream. Take the mold from the freezer and make a second layer with the cherry ice cream. Return to the freezer and, when frozen, make a third layer using the rice pudding. Return the mold to the freezer and continue to freeze.

Sprinkle macaroon crumbs with maraschino liqueur or maraschino cherry liquid and let them stand while the third layer is freezing. When the rice pudding is frozen, add the macaroon crumbs as a fourth layer in the mold. Freeze again. Make a final layer of the remaining vanilla ice cream and freeze.

To unmold, place the mold on a serving plate. Wrap it briefly in a towel that has been dipped in hot water. You will need to repeat this several times. Remove the mold and smooth with a knife if the surface has become slightly liquid. Return to the freezer until serving time. Shortly before serving, whip the cream, adding the sugar and cherry bits while whipping.

To serve, cut the mold like slices of cake so that the layers show. Serve with the whipped cream.

Serves 12.

CHAMPAGNE JELLY

2 packets unflavored gelatin (2 tablespoons)
1/2 cup sugar (or to taste)
1 1/2 cups boiling water
1/2 cup lemon juice
1/2 cup orange juice
1 1/2 cups champagne
garnish: 8 small bunches frosted green grapes
or 8 frosted grapes (optional)

In a medium bowl, mix the gelatin and sugar. Pour in the boiling water and stir until the gelatin is completely dissolved. Add the fruit juices. Stir well. Add the champagne and stir again. Pour into a 1-quart mold or 8 champagne glasses. Chill until firm.

To serve, dip the mold quickly into hot water. (You may have to repeat this if the mold does not loosen.) Turn out onto a serving plate and garnish with frosted grapes. To serve in champagne glasses, garnish each glass with a frosted grape.

Serves 8.

RUSSIAN JELLY

Prepare the ingredients as for champagne jelly. Chill the gelatin in a bowl until almost set. Whip until frothy. Pour into a 1 1/2-quart mold and chill until firm. This jelly will be opaque while the champagne jelly is clear. To serve, dip the mold quickly into hot water. (Dip again, if necessary.) Wipe the mold and turn the contents onto a serving plate. Garnish with frosted green grapes.

Serves 8.

MADEIRA JELLY

2 packets unflavored gelatin (2 tablespoons)
6 tablespoons sugar (or to taste, depending on how
    sweet the wine is)
4 cups Madeira
garnish: 8 small bunches red grapes (optional)

In a medium bowl, mix the gelatin and sugar. Bring the
wine just to a boil. Remove from the heat and pour the wine
into the gelatin and sugar. Stir until the gelatin is completely
dissolved. Chill until partially set. Whip well and return to
the refrigerator. Let set for about 30 minutes longer. Whip
again to a froth. Pour into a 1½-quart mold and chill for
about 2 hours longer.
   To serve, dip the mold quickly into hot water. Wipe the
mold and turn onto a serving plate. Garnish with red grapes,
if desired.

Serves 8.

A hotel advertisement,
1881.

Playing in the sand at Long Branch, 1879. One observer noted that by 1889, Long Branch was no longer "a place a circumspect parent would take his family for a quiet summer by the sea."

FRENCH CREAM MERINGUE

This dessert was served at the Ocean Hotel in Long Branch. It is better known as "floating island."

5 eggs, separated
1/8 teaspoon salt
8 tablespoons sugar
2 cups milk (or half-and-half cream), scalded
1 teaspoon vanilla
currant or raspberry jelly

Combine the egg yolks, salt, and 3 tablespoons of the sugar. Gradually stir in the scalded milk (or cream) and cook over low heat, stirring constantly, until the mixture reaches 175° or lightly coats a metal spoon. Add 1/2 teaspoon of the vanilla. Strain into sherbet glasses or dessert dishes. Chill for several hours.

Beat the egg whites until they froth and form soft peaks. Gradually add the remaining 5 tablespoons of sugar, beating well after each addition. Beat in 1/2 teaspoon vanilla. Spoon a dollop of meringue on each custard. Top with 1/2 teaspoon of currant or raspberry jelly.

Serves 6 to 8.

CARAMEL CUSTARD

This custard was called custard "pudding au caramel" on the hotel menus.

1 cup sugar
1/4 cup water
2 cups each, milk and half-and-half cream
zest of 1 orange
1 2-inch cinnamon stick
6 eggs
2 egg yolks
1 cup sugar
1 teaspoon vanilla

In a small, heavy saucepan, combine the sugar and water. Heat and stir until the sugar dissolves. Do not stir any longer but reduce the heat to moderate when the syrup comes to a boil. Cook briskly until the syrup turns a deep golden brown. Be careful not to scorch it. The syrup may be gently swirled by tipping the pan back and forth. When the desired color is reached, quickly pour about 1 tablespoon of the syrup into each of 8 custard cups. Swirl the syrup around to distribute it over the bottom and sides of the cups. Work quickly. The syrup may be carefully reheated, if necessary.

In a saucepan, heat together the milk, cream, orange zest, and cinnamon until bubbles appear at the edge of the pan. Beat the eggs and egg yolks until foamy. Gradually add the sugar and beat until thick and lemon colored. Remove the cinnamon stick and orange zest from the hot milk. Pour the milk into the egg mixture, stirring constantly. Add the vanilla and strain the custard into a pitcher.

Place the prepared custard cups in a large baking pan and carefully fill them with custard, almost to the top. Set the pan in a 325° oven and fill the pan half full with boiling water. Bake the custards 40 minutes or until a knife inserted in the center comes out clean.

Serves 8.

FRIED CREAM WITH RUM SAUCE

This sweet entrée was often offered as an accompaniment or an alternative to a main dish. It may be served with rum sauce (or currant jelly).

 4 tablespoons flour
 1 tablespoon cornstarch
 1/2 cup sugar
 2 cups milk
 3 egg yolks, lightly beaten
 1 tablespoon butter
 1/2 teaspoon nutmeg
 1 cup bread crumbs
 1 egg, lightly beaten
 oil for frying
 confectioners' sugar

In a medium saucepan, combine the flour, cornstarch, and sugar. Gradually add the milk and stir until smooth. Cook over medium heat until thickened. Stir a small amount of custard into the beaten eggs, mix well, and return the eggs to the milk mixture. Cook, stirring gently, for about 3 minutes more. Beat in the butter and nutmeg. Turn this mixture into a buttered 9x9-inch pan and allow to cool. Cut into 2-inch squares.

Dust each square with crumbs, dip into beaten egg, and again in crumbs. Fry in deep fat at 370° until golden. Dust with confectioners' sugar.

Rum Sauce

 2 egg whites
 1 cup confectioners' sugar
 1/4 cup milk, hot
 3 to 4 tablespoons rum

Beat the egg whites until they hold a soft peak. Add the sugar gradually and continue beating until stiff. Beat in the milk and rum. Serve as a dessert sauce. Yields 1 1/2 cups.

Yields 16 squares.

PEACH FRITTERS WITH ALMOND SAUCE

Peach fritters were served as a sweet entrée.

1/2 cup flour
1/4 teaspoon salt
1 tablespoon butter, melted
1 egg, slightly beaten
1/2 cup beer, flat
1 egg white, stiffly beaten
1 large can cling peaches
oil for frying

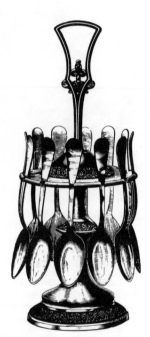

Sift together the flour and salt. Stir in the melted butter and the egg. Gradually stir in the beer, stirring only until smooth. Allow this mixture to set in a warm place for 1 or 2 hours. Just before using, fold in the stiffly beaten egg white.

Drain the peach halves. They may be cut in half if they are too large. Pat them dry, dip into the fritter batter, and fry in deep fat (370°) until golden on each side. Drain them on paper and keep warm for serving. Serve with almond sauce.

Almond Sauce

1/4 cup almonds, slivered
3 tablespoons butter
1/2 cup brown sugar
3/4 cup light corn syrup
3/4 cup light cream
1/2 teaspoon almond extract

Lightly sauté the almonds in the butter. Do not allow them to darken. Add the sugar and corn syrup and cook for 5 minutes. Add the cream and bring to a brisk boil. Stir in the almond extract. Serve hot or cold on peach fritters or ice cream. Yields 2 cups.

Serves 4 to 6.

QUEEN FRITTERS WITH CREAM FILLING

These fritters were served as a sweet entrée dish rather than a dessert.

1 cup water
1/2 cup butter
1/4 teaspoon salt
1 teaspoon sugar
1 cup flour
4 eggs
oil for frying
confectioners' sugar

In a saucepan, place the water, butter, salt, and sugar. Bring to a boil. When the butter has melted add the flour all at once, mixing briskly with a wooden spoon until the dough rolls away from the sides of the pan. Allow this mixture to cool for 5 minutes. Beat in the eggs, one at a time, thoroughly mixing after each addition.

In a heavy saucepan, heat 2 inches of oil to 375°. Drop the dough, 1/2 tablespoon at a time, into the hot oil. Brown on both sides. Drain on paper and allow to cool. Slit each fritter and fill with cream filling. Dust with confectioners' sugar.

Cream Filling

2 tablespoons cornstarch
1/2 cup milk
2 egg yolks, lightly beaten
1 1/2 cups milk
1/4 cup sugar
1/4 teaspoon salt
1/2 teaspoon vanilla
3 teaspoons butter

Stir together the cornstarch and 1/2 cup milk. Add the egg yolks. Heat to a simmer 1 1/2 cups milk, the sugar, and salt. Remove from the heat and whisk in the egg mixture. Return the pan to the heat and cook until thickened. Stir in the vanilla and butter. Press waxed paper onto the surface of the filling and cool.

Yields 24 fritters.

RICE CROQUETTES WITH VANILLA SAUCE

Though preferable today as a dessert, Victorian seaside hotels served rice croquettes with vanilla sauce as an entrée.

2 cups milk
1/2 cup rice
1/4 teaspoon salt
2 egg yolks
3 tablespoons sugar
1/2 teaspoon vanilla
1/2 cup raisins
1 egg
1 tablespoon vegetable oil
1 cup dry bread crumbs
oil for frying

Bring the milk to a boil. Stir in the rice and salt. Cover and reduce the heat. Cook 20 to 30 minutes. Stir occasionally with a fork until the rice is tender. Stir the egg yolks and sugar together and beat into the rice. Add the vanilla and raisins. Spread in an 8 x 8-inch cake pan and chill. When cold, form into pyramids. Beat the egg slightly with 1 tablespoon of oil. Dip the croquettes into the egg, then roll in bread crumbs. Chill 1/2 hour.

Deep fry the croquettes at 375° for 3 to 4 minutes or until golden. Serve with vanilla sauce.

Vanilla Sauce

2 eggs
1/3 cup sugar
dash of salt
1 1/2 cups light cream (or half-and-half cream)
1/2 teaspoon vanilla

In a heavy saucepan, lightly beat the egg yolks and mix in the sugar and salt. Stir in the cream. Cook over low heat, stirring constantly, until the mixture reaches 175° or lightly coats a metal spoon. Stir in the vanilla. Strain and chill. Yields 1 1/2 cups.

Serves 6.

APPLE PUDDING WITH HARD OR BRANDY SAUCE

6 cups apples, peeled and chopped

4 cups medium-sized bread crumbs

3/4 cup brown sugar

1/4 teaspoon salt

2/3 cup butter, melted

1 teaspoon cinnamon

Combine all the ingredients. Pour into a generously buttered, 2-quart baking dish. Bake at 350° for 1 hour and 15 minutes or until the pudding is nicely browned on top. Serve warm with hard or brandy sauce.

Hard Sauce

2/3 cup butter, softened

2 cups confectioners' sugar

1 teaspoon vanilla

1 tablespoon milk

Cream the butter and confectioners' sugar. Add the vanilla and milk. Beat until smooth. Serve cold over apple pudding or other warm puddings. Yields about 1 cup.

Brandy Sauce

Prepare as for hard sauce, but substitute 2 tablespoons of brandy for the vanilla and milk. Yields about 1 cup.

Serves 6 to 8.

CABINET PUDDING WITH ORANGE OR STRAWBERRY SAUCE

Cabinet pudding, also called chancellor's pudding, was an extremely popular hot, sweet dish at the Victorian seaside hotels. Recipes for it appeared in almost every cookbook published during the last half of the nineteenth century.

> 1 cup mixed dried fruit (raisins, apricots, and pears) and/or candied orange peel, lemon peel, and cherries, cut in 1/4-inch dice
> 1/4 cup macaroon crumbs
> 4 tablespoons rum or brandy
> 3 tablespoons sugar
> 12 slices sponge cake (approximately)
> 4 egg yolks
> 1/2 cup sugar
> 2 cups milk
> 1 teaspoon vanilla

Spread the fruit and macaroon crumbs on a plate and sprinkle them with the rum or brandy.

Generously butter a 2-quart pudding mold or deep 2-quart baking dish, and sugar it with the 3 tablespoons of sugar. Arrange the sponge cake slices to cover the bottom of the mold or baking dish. (You will have to break some of the slices.) Sprinkle part of the fruit and macaroon mixture over the sponge cake. Now add a second layer of sponge cake. Top it with more of the fruit and crumb mixture. Continue to layer the cake and fruit until the mold or dish is full, finishing with a layer of cake.

In a large bowl, beat the egg yolks. Add the 1/2 cup of sugar and beat again. Heat the milk just to boiling, stirring constantly. Pour the milk into the eggs and sugar, beating constantly. Add the vanilla and beat again. Slowly pour this custard over the sponge cake. Let it soak in thoroughly and cover with a lid or aluminum foil.

Set the mold or dish into a pan of hot water. The water should come half way up the sides of the dish. Bake at 350° for 1 hour or until a knife inserted in the middle comes out clean. Remove the dish from the water and let it set for 10 minutes. Turn the pudding out onto a serving plate. Serve it warm with orange or strawberry sauce.

Orange Sauce

1/2 cup sugar
2 tablespoons cornstarch
1/8 teaspoon salt
1 1/2 cups orange juice
3 tablespoons lemon juice
1/4 cup butter

In a saucepan, mix the sugar, cornstarch, and salt. Add the juices and cook until the mixture starts to bubble. Simmer over low heat for 4 minutes, stirring constantly. Remove from the heat, add the butter, and stir well. Serve hot. Yields about 2 cups.

Strawberry Sauce

1 1/2 cups crushed strawberries
3/4 cup sugar
3/4 cup currant jelly
1 tablespoon lemon juice
2 tablespoons water
2 tablespoons cornstarch

In a saucepan, combine the strawberries, sugar, and currant jelly. Cook over low heat, stirring constantly, until the mixture bubbles. Make a smooth paste of the water, lemon juice, and cornstarch. Stir the paste into the berry mixture and cook until it is clear and slightly thickened. Yields about 2 cups.

Serves 8 to 10.

The children's playground at the West End Hotel, Long Branch, 1875.

PLUM PUDDING WITH BRANDY OR FAIRY SAUCE

During the Victorian era, plum pudding appeared on the menus of the Jersey Shore hotels not only on Christmas and Thanksgiving but also on Easter and the 4th of July.

1½ cups flour
¾ cup sugar
1 teaspoon salt
¾ teaspoon cinnamon
¼ teaspoon each allspice, cloves, and nutmeg
3 eggs, beaten
1¼ cup ground beef suet
½ cup brandy
1 cup dark raisins
¾ cup golden raisins
¾ cup currants
½ cup dates, chopped
1 cup candied lemon peel, orange peel, and citron, mixed, diced

In a large bowl, mix the flour, sugar, salt, and spices. Add the eggs, suet, and brandy. Mix well. Add the fruits. Mix well. Pour into a well-greased 2-quart pudding mold. Cover tightly. Place the mold on a rack in a kettle. Pour boiling water into the kettle half way up the sides of the mold. Cover the kettle and steam over low heat for 5 hours. (You will have to add more boiling water.)

To serve, turn the pudding out onto a flame-proof serving plate and serve with brandy or fairy sauce. To flame the pudding, pour ¼ cup of heated brandy into a large ladle. Carefully ignite by touching the match to the side of ladle, and then pour the flaming brandy over the plum pudding. This should be done at the table to avoid carrying the lighted dish.

Brandy or Fairy Sauce

2 cups confectioners' sugar
1 cup butter, softened
4 egg yolks, beaten
2 tablespoons brandy

Cream the sugar and butter. Whip in the beaten egg yolks. Cook in a double boiler over lightly boiling water, stirring constantly, until thick enough to coat a wooden spoon. Add the brandy and stir. Serve warm over plum pudding or other warm desserts. For fairy sauce, prepare the ingredients as in brandy sauce, but substitute sherry for the brandy. Yields approximately 1½ cups.

Serves 12.

The Monmouth House, Spring Lake, 1900. Spring Lake began developing as a resort in 1876 with the construction of the Monmouth House. The hotel had 250 "large, well-ventilated rooms, electric calls in every apartment" and was situated between the ocean and the lake.

FARINA PUDDING WITH SHERRY SAUCE

Farina is made from wheat that has had the bran and most of the germ removed. It was thought to be especially digestible.

  2 cups milk
  ½ cup sugar
  2 tablespoons butter
  ¼ teaspoon salt
  4 tablespoons farina
  4 eggs, separated

In a saucepan, combine the milk, sugar, butter, and salt and bring just to the boiling point, stirring constantly. Slowly sprinkle in the farina, stirring constantly, and cook at a gentle boil for 5 minutes. Continue to stir constantly. Remove from the heat and cool.

In a mixing bowl, beat the egg yolks well. Pour the farina mixture into the egg yolks, a little at a time, beating constantly. Beat the egg whites until stiff and gently fold them into the farina mixture. Pour the pudding into a well-buttered, 1½-quart casserole and bake at 350° for 40 minutes. Serve warm with sherry sauce.

Sherry Sauce

  ⅓ cup sugar
  4 teaspoons cornstarch
  ⅛ teaspoon salt
  1 cup water
  4 tablespoons butter
  3 tablespoons cream sherry

In a saucepan, mix the sugar, cornstarch, and salt together. Add the water gradually, stirring to a smooth paste. Cook, stirring constantly, over low heat until the mixture starts to bubble. Continue to cook for 4 minutes over low heat. Remove from the heat and add the butter and sherry. Stir well. Serve hot. Yields 1½ cups.

Serves 6.

RICE PUDDING

Rice pudding was said to have been the favorite dessert of President Ulysses S. Grant, who summered at Long Branch.

1/2 cup rice
2 cups cold water, salted
1 1/4 cups milk
1/2 cup sugar
2 tablespoons butter
4 tablespoons confectioners' sugar (or to taste)
1 teaspoon vanilla
1/2 cup heavy whipping cream
8 maraschino cherries with stems

In a saucepan, boil the rice in the salted water for 20 minutes. Stir often so the rice does not stick to the bottom of the pan.

In the top of a double boiler bring the milk to a slow boil. Add the rice, undrained, and the sugar. Place the milk, rice, and sugar over boiling water and cook for 1 1/4 hours, stirring occasionally. You will have to continue to add boiling water to the bottom of the double boiler. The water should be kept boiling and partially up the sides of the top half of the double boiler. Remove the rice from the heat. Add the butter and stir. Chill the pudding.

Add the confectioners' sugar and vanilla to the whipping cream and whip until it is thick. Fold the cream into the chilled rice. Chill again until serving time.

To serve, spoon the rice pudding into sherbet glasses and top each one with a maraschino cherry.

Serves 8.

◁SEASON 1881▷

CONGRESS HALL,

CAPE MAY, N. J.

H. J. & G. R. CRUMP,

⊢OF COLONNADE HOTEL, PHILADELPHIA⊢

⊣PROPRIETORS.

Replete with all Modern Improvements.

TABLE OF PARTICULAR EXCELLENCE.

LOCATION THE BEST.

An advertisement for the Congress Hall, Cape May, 1881. The earlier wooden version of the Congress Hall burned in 1878. Undaunted by the loss, the proprietors rebuilt the hotel in brick. Of the new dining hall one visitor raved, "What else can it be but grand? At night, when this hall is cleared of its tables and chairs, and hundreds of gas jets are brilliantly burning and flickering and the gay and the elite are flushed with the giddy dance, then you behold a hall-scene, beautiful and fair."

CAKES & PASTRIES

CITRON CAKE

1 cup butter, softened
1 cup sugar
3 tablespoons lemon juice
4 large or 5 medium eggs
1³/₄ cups flour
¹/₂ teaspoon baking powder
¹/₈ teaspoon salt
3 ounces candied citron, chopped medium fine

Cream the butter thoroughly. Add the sugar gradually and beat well. Add the lemon juice and continue to beat. Add the eggs, one at a time, beating well between each addition. Add the flour, baking powder, and salt. Beat thoroughly. Fold in the citron.

Pour the batter into a well-greased and floured 9x5x3-inch loaf pan. Bake at 300° for 1¹/₂ hours or until a cake tester comes out dry. Test at 1¹/₄ hours. Let the cake stand for 10 minutes before turning it out. It should be served at room temperature.

Yields one loaf.

GÂTEAU DE PORTUGAL

6 egg yolks

1½ cups sugar

1 teaspoon baking powder

½ teaspoon salt

1½ cups flour

⅓ cup plus 1 tablespoon orange juice

6 egg whites

½ teaspoon cream of tartar

⅓ cup apricot jam (approximately)

In a mixing bowl, beat the egg yolks until thick. Gradually beat in the sugar. Add the baking powder and salt. Beat well. Add the flour a little at a time, alternating with the orange juice. Beat well between additions. In a large mixing bowl, beat the egg whites and the cream of tartar until stiff. Fold in the sugar, flour, and egg mixture, gently and thoroughly.

Line the bottom of a 9x13-inch baking pan with wax paper. Grease and flour the wax paper and pour in the cake batter. Bake at 325° for 35 to 40 minutes. The top of the cake should spring back when lightly pressed with the fingers.

Remove the cake from the oven. Run a knife around the edges of the cake and turn out at once. Remove the wax paper from the cake. Spread the cake lightly with the apricot jam. (Do not cover the sides.) Allow the cake to cool completely. Spread the sides and top of the cake with orange butter icing.

Orange Butter Icing

¼ cup butter, softened

2 cups confectioners' sugar

2 tablespoons orange juice

Mix all of the ingredients together thoroughly and spread on the cake.

Serves 12 to 15.

NELSON CAKE

Nelson cake was traditionally served cold, but it is also delicious warm.

- 1 sheet puff pastry (commercial frozen variety is excellent)
- 2 tablespoons butter, very soft
- 1/2 cup raisins or currants
- 1/4 cup sugar
- 1/2 teaspoon cinnamon
- 1 tablespoon lemon juice
- 1 teaspoon water

Roll the puff pastry into a 10x12-inch sheet. Cut it in half to make 2 sheets of pastry 10x6 inches. Prick with a fork all over. Spread each sheet of pastry with 1 tablespoon of butter.

Soak the raisins or currants in water for 10 minutes. Drain but do not dry them. Arrange the raisins or currants evenly over one of the pastry sheets. Sprinkle the sugar over the fruit. Sprinkle the cinnamon over the sugar. Mix the lemon juice and water and sprinkle it over the cinnamon. Now put the second layer of pastry over the first, the buttered sides together.

Place the cake on an ungreased cookie sheet. Bake at 350° for 20 minutes. Take the cake from the oven and move it around on the cookie sheet to make sure it has not stuck. Ice the cake while it is still warm. Allow the cake to cool. Move the cake carefully to a serving plate and cut it with a sharp, serrated knife.

Icing for Nelson Cake

- 3/4 cup confectioners' sugar
- 1 tablespoon boiling water
- 2 drops vanilla
- dash of salt.

In a small mixing bowl, combine all the ingredients and mix them well.

Serves 8.

COCONUT CAKE

2/3 cup butter

1 1/2 cups sugar

3 eggs

2 1/4 cups flour, sifted

2 1/2 teaspoons baking powder

1 teaspoon salt

1 cup milk

1 1/2 teaspoons vanilla

Cream together the butter and sugar. Beat in the eggs, one at a time, and beat until fluffy. Sift together the flour, baking powder, and salt. Alternately by thirds, stir the dry ingredients and the milk into the butter and sugar. Stir in the vanilla. Pour the batter into 2 greased and floured 8-inch layer pans and bake at 350° for 25 to 30 minutes. Allow the cake to set in the pans for 5 minutes, then turn the layers out onto cake racks and cool. The coconut cake will be assembled with lemon filling and whipped cream.

Lemon Filling

1/2 cup sugar

2 tablespoons cornstarch

3/4 cup water

2 large egg yolks

1 tablespoon butter

2 teaspoons lemon rind, grated

1/4 cup lemon juice

In a saucepan, stir together the sugar and cornstarch. Gradually stir in the water until a smooth paste is formed. Beat in the egg yolks until well blended. Cook over medium heat until the mixture bubbles and thickens. Remove from the heat and stir in the butter, lemon rind, and juice. Place in a bowl and cover with plastic wrap. Chill thoroughly.

Whipped Cream

1 cup heavy cream

1 tablespoon sugar

1 teaspoon vanilla

Beat the cream in a chilled bowl until it begins to thicken. Add the sugar and vanilla and beat until thick.

Assembling the Cake

**Fresh coconut, shredded (or canned if fresh
   is unavailable)**

Lay 3 strips of waxed paper on a cake plate to form a triangle. Place one cake layer, top down, in the center of the triangle. The paper will protect the cake plate from excess frosting and coconut. Smooth the lemon filling over the layer and place the second layer, top up, in place. Frost the top and sides with whipped cream. Press the coconut generously over the frosting. Gently brush the excess coconut from the waxed paper and carefully remove the paper from under the cake. Refrigerate until served.

Yields 1 8-inch 2-layer cake.

APPLE MERINGUE PIE

**6 to 7 cups green apple slices (about 8 medium-
   sized apples, peeled)**
1½ cups sugar
½ teaspoon nutmeg
¼ cup butter
¼ teaspoon salt
1 tablespoon lemon juice
1 9-inch pie shell, baked

In a saucepan, combine the apples, sugar, nutmeg, butter, salt, and lemon juice. (If you use ripe apples, reduce the sugar to 1 cup and add 1 teaspoon of cinnamon.) Cover and cook over low heat until the apples are soft. Mash and continue to cook until the apples are as dry as possible without scorching. You will have to stir often and watch carefully. Allow to cool.

Pour the apples into the pie shell and cover with meringue. Bake at 400° for 8 to 10 minutes.

Meringue

3 egg whites
¼ teaspoon cream of tartar
6 tablespoons sugar

Beat the egg whites and cream of tartar to a froth. Gradually beat in the sugar. Continue to beat until stiff.

Yields 1 9-inch pie.

APRICOT PIE

This is a very rich pie, so servings should be small.

4 ounces dried apricots (to yield ¾ cup apricot pulp)
½ cup butter
2 cups sugar
½ teaspoon salt
4 eggs, beaten
1 tablespoon lemon juice
1 9-inch pie shell, unbaked

Wash the apricots and cook until very soft, according to the directions on the package. Drain and mash well. To the apricot pulp add the butter, sugar, salt, eggs, and lemon juice. Mix well.

Pour the apricot into the pie shell and bake at 350° for 55 minutes.

Yields 1 9-inch pie.

A hotel advertisement, 1890.

GRAPE PIE

Concord grapes were popular in New Jersey. This is a most delicious and different way to use them.

- **5 cups Concord grapes**
- **1 cup sugar**
- **4 tablespoons flour**
- **1 teaspoon lemon juice**
- **1 lemon rind, grated**
- **1 9-inch pie shell and top, unbaked**
- **1½ tablespoons butter**
- **1 tablespoon milk**
- **1 tablespoon sugar**

Slip the skins from the grapes and reserve them. Place the pulp in a saucepan and cook until it comes to a boil. Rub the pulp through a strainer to remove the seeds. Mix the pulp with the reserved skins.

Combine the sugar and flour. Toss lightly with the grapes, lemon, and lemon rind. Fill the pie shell and dot with butter. Top the pie with a lattice crust. Bake at 425° for 35 to 45 minutes. When the filling begins to bubble and the crust is light tan, brush the lattice with milk, and sprinkle it with sugar. Bake 5 minutes longer or until golden.

Yields 1 9-inch pie.

Dancing the Lancers at Cape May, 1871. "It is no uncommon experience for the belles and beaux of the ball-room to make appointments between the figures of the Lancers for the next day's bath."

CONFECTIONS

ALMOND PRALINES

This is the French praline, rather than the New Orleans adaptation that we know as pralines in America today. Pralines take their name from a seventeenth-century French nobleman, César du Plessis-Praslin, who believed them to be an aid to digestion.

1 cup almonds, blanched
1 cup sugar
1/3 cup water
1 tablespoon butter
1/4 teaspoon salt
1/4 teaspoon vanilla flavoring

Spread the almonds in a large pan or skillet. Make a syrup by combining the sugar, water, butter, and salt in a heavy saucepan. Bring to a boil, stirring constantly until the sugar is dissolved. Continue to boil until the syrup reaches 240° on a candy thermometer (the soft ball stage, when a small amount of syrup dropped in cold water forms a soft ball).

Remove the syrup from the heat, stir in the vanilla, and pour half the syrup quickly over the almonds. Stir very quickly and vigorously until each nut is separate and coated. Wait 3 minutes. Pour the remaining syrup over the coated nuts, stirring quickly and vigorously to add a second coat of sugar to each nut.

Yields 2 cups.

CHOCOLATE KISSES

1/2 cup cake flour, sifted
3/4 cup sugar
4 egg whites
1/4 teaspoon salt
4 ounces semi-sweet chocolate, melted
1/2 teaspoon vanilla

Sift together the flour and 1/4 cup of sugar. Beat the egg whites with the salt until soft peaks form. Gradually beat in the remaining sugar, 2 tablespoons at a time, until very stiff. Fold in the flour mixture, 1/4 cup at a time. Fold in the chocolate and vanilla. Drop from a teaspoon, or press from a pastry bag with a large star tube, onto a paper-lined or lightly greased cookie sheet. Bake at 270° for 40 to 50 minutes.

Yields 24 kisses.

COCONUT KISSES

Condensed milk was patented in 1856 by Mr. Gail Borden. It lent itself to various uses and newly devised recipes. These kisses were served in 1872 at the Mansion House in Long Branch.

1 can condensed milk (14 ounces)
3 cups coconut, shredded

Mix the condensed milk and coconut together. Drop by the teaspoonful onto ungreased brown paper or bakers' parchment placed on a cookie sheet. Bake at 350° for 12 to 14 minutes. Be careful the kisses do not burn on the bottom. Cool slightly and remove to a cooling rack.

Yields 30 kisses.

TURKISH DELIGHT

2 cups sugar

1 cup water

2 tablespoons white corn syrup

1/2 teaspoon salt

1/3 cup lemon juice

1/3 cup orange juice

3 packets unflavored gelatin

3 drops of red or green food coloring
  (more, if desired)

1/3 cup confectioners' sugar, sifted

1/2 cup chopped nuts (optional)

additional confectioners' sugar

Make a syrup by combining the sugar, water, corn syrup, and salt in a saucepan. Stir and bring to a boil. Let the syrup boil gently for 40 minutes or until it reaches 240° on a candy thermometer (the soft ball stage). Remove it from the heat. There should be 1 1/2 cups.

Pour the lemon and orange juices into a small bowl. Sprinkle the gelatin on the top of the juices and let it sit until the gelatin is dissolved. Stir the gelatin mixture into the syrup. Add the food coloring and stir until the gelatin is dissolved and well blended. Place the confectioners' sugar in a bowl. Add the gelatin mixture slowly and stir until the sugar is dissolved and well blended. Stir in the nuts, if desired.

Sprinkle a thin layer of confectioners' sugar on the bottom of a 6x8-inch baking dish. Pour in the gelatin mixture. (It will be about 1 inch thick.) Sift a thin layer of confectioners' sugar onto the top. Allow it to set, approximately 4 hours. Cut into 1-inch squares with a sharp knife. Roll in confectioners' sugar.

Yields 48 pieces.

OCEAN HOTEL WINES.

Champagnes.

	PTS.	QTS.
Veuve Clicquot, Yellow Label	$ 2 00	$4 00
Pommery Sec	2 00	4 00
G. H. Mumm's Extra Dry	2 00	4 00
Piper Heidsieck	1 75	3 50
Dry Monopole	2 00	4 00
Delmonico	1 75	3 50
L. Roederer's Carte Blanche	2 00	4 00

Clarets.

Vin Ordinaire	40	80
Medoc	50	1 00
Floriac	65	1 25
St. Estephe	75	1 50
St. Julien	1 00	2 00
Pontet Canet	1 25	2 50
Chateau La Rose	1 25	2 50
Chateau Martinens, 1877		3 00
Chateau Lafite, 1874	1 75	3 50
Chateau Margaux, 1874	2 00	4 00

Sauternes.

Graves	75	1 50
Barsac	75	1 50
Bommes	1 25	2 50
La Tour Blanche	1 25	2 50
Haut Sauternes	1 25	2 50
Chateau Yquem, 1874	2 00	4 00

Burgundy.

Macon	75	1 50
Nuits	1 50	3 00
Chambertin	1 50	3 00
" 1865, pints only	2 00	
Clos de Vougeot		4 00
Chablis (white)	75	1 50
Hermitage (white)		3 50

Rhine Wines.

Laubenheimer		1 00
Hochheimer		1 50
Geisenheimer		2 00
Rudesheimer		3 00
Steinberger, Cabinet		3 50
Johannisberger (Schloss)		4 00

American Wines.

Still Catawba	50	1 00
California Hock	50	1 00

Sherry.

Table	90	1 50
Topaz	1 00	2 00
Cabinet	1 25	2 50
Montilla	1 50	3 00
Amontillado	2 00	4 00
Old Solera	2 50	5 00

Madeira.

	PTS.	QTS.
Old East India	$2 50	$5 00
Victoria Royal	1 50	3 00
Ivanhoe	2 00	4 00

Port.

Old Port	1 00	2 00
London Dock	1 25	2 50
White Port	2 00	4 00
Sandeman, Pure Juice	1 50	3 00

Whiskies, Brandies, Etc.

Union Club Rye	2 00
Kentucky Valley Bourbon	2 00
Private Stock Cabinet	3 00
Hennessey S. O. P	3 00
" V. S. O. P	5 00
" 1848	7 00
Blackberry Brandy	2 00
Monmouth Apple Jack	2 00
Holland Gin	2 00
Old Tom Gin	2 00
St. Croix, Royal Crown	2 50
Jamaica Rum, London Club	3 00

Cordials and Liqueurs.

Vermouth	per glass 20
Chartreuse	20
Curacoa	20
Maraschino or Anisette	20
Kirschwasser	20
Absinthe	20
Benedictine	20
Kummel	20

Ales, Porters, Etc.

New York Lager Beer	15
Milwaukee Lager	20
" Export Beer	25
Clausen's Champagne Lager	20
Imported Tivoli Beer	40
" Kaiser Beer	30
" Culmbach	30
Bass' Ale, India Pale	30
" White Label	30
Muir's Scotch Ale	30
Guinness' Stout	30
Ginger Ale, C. & C., Belfast	25
Cider (extra), pint, 30c.; quart	60

Mineral Waters, Etc.

Apollinaris	25	40
Clysmic		40
Congress	25	40
Hathorn	25	
Syphon Seltzer, C. S.		25
Syphon Vichy, "		25
Syphon Carbonic		25
Hunyadi Water	40	

The wine and liquor list from the Ocean Hotel, Long Branch, August 27, 1884. (Courtesy, Special Collections, Alexander Library, Rutgers University)

BEVERAGES

LALLA ROOKH

This drink was named for the heroine created by the poet Thomas Moore in 1817. The New York version of Lalla Rookh was a dessert made with half of a cantaloupe filled with orange sherbet and 1 tablespoon of liqueur poured over the sherbet. The Philadelphia Lalla Rookh, however, was a punch. This version was served before the roast course at the Jersey Shore hotels during the Victorian era.

8 egg yolks
1 cup sugar
4 cups milk
3/4 cup heavy whipping cream
1/4 cup brandy
1/3 cup rum
nutmeg

In a mixing bowl, beat the egg yolks. Add the sugar a little at a time. Beat well. In a saucepan heat the milk just to the boiling point, stirring constantly. Pour the milk, a little at a time, into the egg and sugar mixture, stirring constantly. Return the milk mixture to the saucepan and continue to cook, stirring constantly, until the mixture reaches 175° on a candy thermometer. Pour into a bowl and chill.

Whip the cream until it is stiff. Fold the cream into the chilled milk mixture until it is mixed well. Place it in the freezer until it starts to freeze.

Add the brandy and rum. Stir well. Whip for about 30 seconds. Sprinkle with nutmeg. Serve in punch cups.

Serves 12.

CLARET PUNCH

Claret is the traditional English name for Bordeaux wine. Any dry red table wine may be used in this punch.

3/4 cup sugar
1/4 cup lemon juice
1/4 cup orange liqueur
sprig of mint leaves
2 bottles dry red wine
1 bottle soda water (32 ounces)
block of ice

In a punch bowl, mix the sugar, lemon juice, and orange liqueur. Add the sprig of mint. Let stand for an hour or so. Remove the mint sprig. Add the wine and soda water. Stir and chill well. Just before serving stir again and add the block of ice. Serve in punch cups.

Serves 24.

ROMAN PUNCH

Roman punch was a favorite Victorian drink, served between the first and second service of dinner. It was usually served just before the roast or game course. The drink's only connection with Rome, people said in jest, was that it could have been served at an orgy.

1 quart lemon sherbet
1/2 cup orange liqueur
2 bottles champagne, cold

Place the sherbet into a punch bowl and let it soften. Add the orange liqueur and stir it into the softened sherbet. Pour the champagne gently over it. Stir gently but well. Serve in punch cups.

Serves 24.

ROMAN PUNCH IN ORANGE CUPS

During President Rutherford B. Hayes's administration (1877–81), alcoholic beverages were banned from the White House, much to the consternation of many Washington politicians and diplomats. The First Lady earned the sobriquet "Lemonade Lucy." Roman punch in orange cups was served in the Hayes White House, but non-alcoholic rum flavoring was used.

10 to 12 oranges (depending on size)
1 quart lemon sherbet
1 cup rum

Cut the top third from each orange. Scoop out the inside, leaving the hollow shell. Soften the sherbet. Mix it with the rum. Spoon the mixture into the orange shells. Place the shells in the freezer for 1/2 hour. The sherbet should be firm but not frozen hard. Serve at once. It should be eaten with a spoon.

Serves 10 to 12.

United States Hotel, Long Branch, 1858.

INDEX

Almond: pralines, 145; sauce, 126; zwieback, 111
Anchovy sauce, 38
Apple: meringue pie, 141–42; pudding with hard or brandy sauce, 129; sauce for duck, 49
Apricot pie, 142

Bass. *See* Sea bass
Beef: boiled, 62–63; bouillon, 9; bouillon, jellied, 10; brunoise, 11; corned, 60; corned, and cabbage, 60; gravy, for boiled beef, 63; oxtail soup, 14; porterhouse steak with onions, 58; ragoût parisienne, 61; standing rib roast with Yorkshire pudding, 59; tenderloin of, à la jardiniere, 55; tenderloin of, bordelaise, 56–57; tongue, 64, 65
Beverages: claret punch, 150; Lalla Rookh, 149; Roman punch, 150; Roman punch in orange cups, 151
Biscuits, 107; raised, 112; short, 108
Blancmange, 117
Blanquette of veal, 76
Bluefish, broiled, maître d'hôtel, 27
Boiled beef, 62–63
Bordelaise, sauce, 53, 56–57
Bouillon: beef, 9; jellied beef, 10; tomato, 25
Brandy sauce, 129, 133
Bread griddlecakes, 108
Bread: *(quick)* almond zwieback, 111; biscuits, 107; corn bread, 109; popovers, 110; short biscuits, 108. *(yeast)* breakfast rolls, 113; entire wheat bread, 114; Graham bread, 115; raised biscuits, 112
Brunoise, 11
Butter maître d'hôtel, 27

Cabbage, corned beef and, 60
Cabinet pudding with orange or strawberry sauce, 130–31
Cake: citron, 137; coconut, 140; gâ-teau de Portugal, 138; Nelson, 139
Candied sweet potatoes, 103
Caper sauce, 73
Caramel custard, 124
Cauliflower soup, cream of, 24
Champagne: jelly, 121; sauce, 84
Charlotte russe, 118
Chicken: à la reine, 20; consommé, 16–19; gumbo, 15; liver with Madeira sauce, 46; Marengo, 42–43; quenelles, 45; rissolé, 44; with curry-raisin sauce, 41–42. *See also* Fowl
Chocolate kisses, 146
Chowder, clam, with tomatoes, 23
Cinnamon sauce, 84
Citron cake, 137
Clam: broth, 22; chowder with tomatoes, 23; fritters, 36; soup, 22–23
Claret punch, 150
Coconut: cake, 140; kisses, 146
Confections: almond pralines, 145; chocolate kisses, 146; coconut kisses, 146; Turkish delight, 147
Consommé: à la royale, 16; brunoise, 11; chicken, 16; Colbert, 17; julienne, 17; princess, 18; tapioca, 18; vermicelli, 19
Corn bread, 109
Corn O'Brien, 89
Corned beef, 60; and cabbage, 60
Crabs, soft-shell, with cresson sauce, 37
Cream: filling for queen fritters, 127; fried, with rum sauce, 125; whipped, 140; of cauliflower soup, 24; of oyster soup, 21
Cresson sauce, 37
Croquettes: potato, 91, 92; potatoes en surprise, 93; rice, with vanilla sauce, 128
Currant jelly sauce, 74
Custard: caramel, 124; French cream meringue, 123; fried cream with rum sauce, 125
Cutlets: lamb, breaded, with tomato sauce, 70–71; lobster, with anchovy sauce, 38

Desserts. *See* Cake; Custard; Fritters; Frozen desserts; Gelatins; Pie; Pudding
Dressing for roast suckling pig, 87
Duck: salmis of, with olives, 48; spring, with apple sauce, 49

Egg sauce, 28
Entire wheat bread, 114

Fairy sauce, 133
Farina pudding with sherry sauce, 134
Filling: cream, 127; lemon, 140
Fish: bluefish, broiled, maître d'hôtel, 27; haddock, boiled, with egg sauce, 28; halibut, baked, with port sauce, 29; quenelles, 45; salmon poached, with lobster or oyster sauce, 30–31; sea bass, baked, with sauce normande, 32–33; stock, 33
Floating island, 123
Fowl, boiled, with sauce suprême, 46–47
Frascati glacé, 119
French cream meringue, 123
Fricandeau of veal with green peas, 80–81
Fricassée of veal, 77
Fried cream with rum sauce, 125
Fritters: clam, 36; peach, with almond sauce, 126; queen, with cream filling, 127
Frozen desserts: frascati glacé, 119; maraschino cream imperial, 120

Gâteau de Portugal, 138
Gelatins: champagne jelly, 121; Charlotte russe, 118; Madeira jelly, 122; Russian jelly, 121
Graham bread, 115
Grape pie, 143
Gravy: brown, 75; for boiled beef, 63; for roast suckling pig, 87
Green peppers, stuffed, 90
Griddlecakes. *See* Bread griddlecakes
Gumbo, chicken, 15

Haddock, boiled, with egg sauce, 28
Halibut, baked, with port sauce, 29
Ham: baked, 83; boiled, 83; glazed, cold, 85
Hard sauce, 129
Hashed potatoes in cream, 96
Herb stuffing, for veal, 78

Icing: for Nelson cake, 139; orange butter, 138

Jellied beef bouillon, 10
Jelly. *See* Gelatins

Lalla Rookh, 149
Lamb: chops Maintenon, 68–69; cutlets, breaded, with tomato sauce, 70–71; pie, 66–67; roast leg, with mint sauce, 67. *See also* Mutton
Lemon filling, 140
Liver, chicken, with Madiera sauce, 46
Lobster: cutlets with anchovy sauce, 38; salad, 39; sauce, 31
Long Branch, potatoes, 95

Madeira: jelly, 122; sauce, 84
Maraschino cream imperial, 120
Marengo, chicken, 42–43
Marsala sauce, 85
Mashed potato salad, 99
Meringue, 142
Mint sauce, 67
Mock turtle soup, 12–13
Mustard, 63
Mutton, boiled leg, with caper sauce or sauce vénitienne, 72–73

Nelson cake, 139
Normande, sauce, 33

Olives, 48
Onions: creamed, 100; fried, 58
Orange butter icing, 138
Orange sauce, 131
Oxtail soup, 14
Oyster(s): on the half-shell, 34; sauce, 31; scalloped, 35; soup, cream of, 21

Pastry, for lamb pie, 66–67
Peach fritters with almond sauce, 126
Pie: apple meringue, 141–42; apricot, 142; grape, 143; lamb, 66–67
Plum pudding with brandy or fairy sauce, 132–33
Popovers, 110
Pork. *See* Ham; Roast suckling pig
Porterhouse steak with onions, 58

Potato(es): château, 94; croquettes, 91, 92; en surprise, 93; hashed, in cream, 96; hollandaise, 96; Long Branch, 95; new, in cream, 97; salad, 98; salad, mashed, 99; Saratoga chips, 95
Poultry. *See* Chicken; Duck; Fowl; Squab
Pralines, almond, 145
Pudding: apple, with hard or brandy sauce, 129; cabinet, with orange or strawberry sauce, 130–31; farina, with sherry sauce, 134; plum, with brandy or fairy sauce, 132—33; rice, 135; Yorkshire, 59
Punch. *See* Beverages

Queen fritters with cream filling, 127
Quenelles, 45

Ragoût of beef parisienne, 61
Rib roast of beef with Yorkshire pudding, 59
Rice croquettes with vanilla sauce, 128
Rice pudding, 135
Rissolé of chicken, 44
Roast: leg of lamb with mint sauce, 67; loin of veal, 75; shoulder of veal with herb stuffing, 78–79; squab maître d'hôtel, 50–51; standing ribs, beef, 59; suckling pig, 86–87
Rolls, breakfast, 113
Roman punch, 150; in orange cups, 151
Rum sauce, 125
Russian jelly, 121

Salad: lobster, 39; mashed potato, 99; potato, 98
Salmis of duck with olives, 48
Salmon, poached, with lobster or oyster sauce, 30–31
Saratoga chips, 95
Sauce: *(for fish)* anchovy, 38; butter maître d'hôtel, 27; cresson, 37; egg, 28; lobster, 31; normande, 33; oyster, 31. *(for meat)* bordelaise, 56–57; caper, 73; champagne, 84; cinnamon, 84; currant jelly, 74; Madeira, 84; Marsala, 85; mint, 67; sultana, 64; tomato, 71, 79; vénitienne, 73. *(for poultry)* apple, 49; bordelaise, 53; suprême, 47; thick white, 44. *(sweet)* almond, 126; brandy, 129, 133; fairy, 133; hard, 129; orange, 131; rum, 125; sherry, 134; strawberry, 131; vanilla, 128

Sea bass, baked, with sauce normande, 32–33
Seafood. *See* Clams; Crabs; Fish; Lobster; Oyster(s)
Sherry sauce, 134
Short biscuits, 108
Soft-shell crabs with cresson sauce, 37
Soup: clam, 22–23; clam broth, 22; clam chowder with tomatoes, 23; chicken à la reine, 20; chicken gumbo, 15; cream of cauliflower, 24; cream of oyster, 21; mock turtle, 12–13; oxtail, 14. *See also* Bouillon; Consommé
Spring duck with apple sauce, 49
Squab: bordelaise, 53; roast, maître d'hôtel, 50–51
Stock: fish, 33; veal, 12
Strawberry sauce, 131
Stuffing: for squab, 51; herb, for veal, 78
Suckling pig, roast, 86–87
Sultana sauce, 64
Suprême, sauce, 47
Sweetbreads, veal, in puff pastry, 82
Sweet entrées: fried cream with rum sauce, 125; peach fritters with almond sauce, 126; queen fritters with cream filling, 127; rice croquettes with vanilla sauce, 128
Sweet potatoes: browned, 102; candied, 103

Tenderloin: of beef à la jardiniere, 55; of beef with sauce bordelaise, 56–57
Tomato(es): bouillon, 25; sauce, 71, 77; scalloped, 104; stewed, 104–5; stuffed, 105
Tongue, beef, 64, 65
Turkish delight, 147
Turtle soup. *See* Mock turtle soup

Vanilla sauce, 128
Veal: balls, 12, blanquette of, 76; fricandeau of, with peas, 80–81; fricassée of, 77; loin roast, 75; mock turtle soup, 12–13; quenelles, 45; shoulder, with herb stuffing, 78–79; stock, 12; sweetbreads in puff pastry, 82
Venison steaks with currant jelly, 74
Vénitienne, sauce, 73

Whipped cream, 140
White sauce, thick, 44

Yorkshire pudding, 59

Zwieback, almond, 111